Big Lessons
from
Little Places

Faithfulness
and the Future
in Small
Congregations

Big Lessons from Little Places

Faithfulness and the Future in Small Congregations

KAY COLLIER McLAUGHLIN

Morehouse Publishing
NEW YORK

Unless otherwise noted, the Scripture quotations contained herein are from the New Revised Standard Version Bible, copyright © 1989 by the Division of Christian Education of the National Council of Churches of Christ in the U.S.A. Used by permission. All rights reserved.

Morehouse Publishing, 19 East 34th Street, New York, NY 10016
Morehouse Publishing is an imprint of Church Publishing Incorporated.
www.churchpublishing.org

Cover design by Laurie Klein Westhafer
Typeset by Beth Oberholtzer

Library of Congress Cataloging-in-Publication Data

Collier McLaughlin, Kay.
   Big lessons from little places : faithfulness and the future in small
congregations / Kay Collier McLaughlin.
      pages   cm
   Includes bibliographical references.
   ISBN 978-0-8192-3167-3 (pbk.) — ISBN 978-0-8192-3168-0 (ebook)
   1. Small churches.   2. Pastoral theology.   3. Episcopal Church.   I. Title.
BV637.8.C65   2015
253—dc23
                                                              2014042797

Printed in the United States of America

*To the congregations of the Diocese of Lexington
who have been my teachers and examples
of "Lessons in Faithfulness"
and to the Kingdom Come Parkway
and its enduring inspiration in my life*

In this He showed me a little thing; the quantity of a
hazelnut, lying in the palm of my hand, and to my
understanding, it was as round as any ball. I looked
thereupon and thought: 'What may this be?' And
I was answered in a general way, thus. 'It is all
that is made.' I marveled how it could last, for
me thought it might fall suddenly to naught for littleness.
And I was answered in my understanding: 'It lasts
and ever shall last because God loves it and so hath all
things its being through the love of God.

JULIAN OF NORWICH[1]

———————
1. Quoted in Fae Malania, *The Quality of a Hazelnut* (New York: Alfred A. Knopf, 1968).

Contents

The Road to Kingdom Come

I have traveled the Kingdom Come Parkway. I have traveled it with Kay Collier McLaughlin, with whom I worked in the Diocese of Lexington for the most spiritually rewarding years of my life. I have traveled it with many others. Most importantly, though, I have traveled it alone.

I often ask myself how exactly I turned on it to begin with. It was neither my intended destination nor route. God had other ideas. For some reason, so did the people of the Diocese of Lexington when they called me to be their bishop, surprising me as much as anyone, and I suspect surprising even themselves.

They taught me so many things about leadership, the Gospel, faith, fear, and love. They also taught me about small churches, of which I had virtually no experience and only a little appreciation when I took up my new ministry fourteen years ago.

The first thing I learned was that, although I was always greeted politely and warmly (well, there were some exceptions in the midst of controversies in our church around 2003), I was also feared. "The bishop is going to close us," I learned, was a pervasive assumption. I had never said that. I really hadn't even thought that. Still, that was the fear. It wasn't personal at all. It existed long before I got there, but I hope may be less likely to exist now.

That is the origin of the Hot Dog Fund I found in one small congregation. Its existence had gone unnoticed in the annual audit year after year, despite a balance of several thousand dollars. Eventually, I asked. With some embarrassment, the leadership explained the fund had been named so that the bishop wouldn't notice it was there. It was only after a number of trips up and down the Kingdom Come Parkway that I came to understand that the road to Kingdom Come is about being liberated from the fear of not surviving. It is only when you risk the Hot Dog Fund that life in abundance becomes possible.

One of the things that concern me most about the life of the Church right now is its anxious concern for survival. It is something that churches of all sizes have in common. It is something small churches especially have that is important to teach because they have fewer pretenses for denial. It would behoove all of us well to listen. That is what this very important book is about.

One of the most important things I learned from small churches in Eastern Kentucky is that, once they were freed from the fear of survival and the suspicion that the bishop really only wanted to close them so that he could take the Hot Dog Fund, they could take risks of faith, even ones that put survival at risk. And as they did, they found the life we are all promised. The way of life is the way of the cross, and that leaves no room for survival. Small churches live in that reality in a way others do not. But others eventually will, and they have the gift of learning from small churches now, before it's too late. Small churches can show us how to find life beyond survival, the life Jesus promised, precisely because they have lived closer to the boundaries of survival than most.

The priest at one of our smallest congregations once told me about stopping to fill up his car while wearing his collar. "What church are you with?" the cashier asked.

"St. Philip's," he answered.

"Oh, is that the church with the big sanctuary?" the cashier, who obviously wanted to know more, inquired.

"No, that's the Baptist Church."

"Then it must be the church with the big gym?" was the conclusion.

"No," the priest explained, somewhat discouraged. "That's the Methodist Church."

"The one with the big Wednesday night program."

Wrong again. "That's the Church of God."

Finally, the cashier got it. "Oh, I know. You're the church that feeds people." He was referring to a program that fed anyone who showed up close to the end of each month before the next month's government check arrived when money was running short. There's a lot more that could be said about that feeding program and what it meant in the community, but the point here is what it meant to the church itself, how it stretched the congregation, and how it opened up some important lessons about life for all of us because it distracted Christians from worrying about survival by risking the Hot Dog Fund.

Here's the thing. What St. Philip's did in responding to the needs of the poor in its community was in no way a growth strategy. It was a discipleship strategy. It was a discipleship strategy made all the more important because St. Philip's was the only church in its small community where some people, like gay people or the couple I met who were no longer welcome in their previous church because they were divorced and remarried or drug addicts or alcoholics, could conceivably be accepted.

What I began to learn as Bishop of Lexington was how important small churches were to proclaiming good news even if they weren't going to have impressive numbers. Even more importantly, what I learned was how important they were to me in hearing good news. What they were for me, thankfully, was an invitation to take a detour onto the road to Kingdom Come. God only knows where I might have ended up without them.

This book is an invitation to you written by someone who knows what she is talking about because she brings the vantage point of someone who continues to study something she has lived all her life. Hers is an authentic voice. It is an appreciative voice. It is a loving voice.

I can only hope it calls you, too, onto the road to Kingdom Come.

Stacy F. Sauls
September 14, 2014
New York City

Acknowledgments

- To members of small congregations who have modeled faithfulness throughout the years, welcomed me to their pulpits, altars, and their hearts, and whose conversations over wonderful pot lucks and coffee hours around the table have turned me toward conversations across our Church, resulting in this book

- To the bishops, priests, deacons, and lay people whose heart for small churches and the future of our Church have enabled hours of helpful conversations

- To the Venerable Bryant Kibler, who has faithfully served more small churches than most can count, and has never failed to roll up his sleeves and go where God calls

- To members of the Diocesan Leadership Team and Shepherding teams, who have tirelessly traveled these byways and embraced each congregation as their own

- To the Network for Pastoral Leadership and Sustaining Healthy Congregations: Richard, Bruce, Tim, Cindy, Janey, Chris, Dominic, Coke, Peter D., Joe, Marshall, Chana, Peter H., Rebecca, TJ, and Amanda and the adventure of flying the airplane as we continue to build it

- To the Small Church Ministry Consortium and those in-between: Margaret, Duane, Lisa, Keila, Sister Judy, Paul, Sandy, Elise, Chris, Carol, Amy, and Mary

- To those risk takers and visionaries through the years who have challenged me, stretched me, stimulated my imagination, and kept me learning and risking with them: Dr. Marvin J. Rabin, the Rev. Joel P. Henning, the Very Rev. Dr. Robert Insko, Bill L. Jett, LCSW, the Rev. William Yon, the Rt. Rev. Stacy Sauls, the Most Rev. Ed Browning, the Rev. Michael "Corky" Carlisle, the Rev. Bruce Stewart, Madeleine L'Engle, Margaret Wheatley, John and Joyce Weir, Dr. Roy Persons, Dr. John Schneider, the Rt. Rev. Chilton Knudsen, and Dr. Pearl Rutledge

- To Karl Vaters and newsmallchurch.com for renewed insight and inspiration

- To all of the unnamed small churches of all denominations that dot the landscape of our country even today, who live in the shadows of the megachurches, continuing their faithful witness for the Kingdom

- To Sharon Ely Pearson and Nancy Bryan for catching the view from the Kingdom Come Parkway

- To my family, without whose love and support nothing would be possible

- To my sister Jane, whose death in the midst of this project claimed the one who walked with me on this and every project of my life—writing permission letters, sharing meals and conversations from my writing hideaways, and whose faithfulness and deep investment in her own beloved St. John's continues to inspire me

- And to my pilgrim band: Whitty, Carolyn, Nan, Jan, Jane, Mary-Louise, Ann, Margaret, Ginger, and Pearl

Introduction

*As a town, we
had made the error
of staying small—and there
is no more unforgivable
crime in America.*

PAT CONROY,
THE PRINCE OF TIDES[1]

"Would you be willing to share more of what is happening in your congregation?" The Presiding Bishop of the Episcopal Church was singling out the man who had spoken to the Episcopal Church's Executive Council about the smallest congregation in the host diocese for the meeting. What did Ed Browning know that propelled his focus on the man from this church—which by levels of church measurement would fall into the "family" sized designation—under fifty people in attendance on average Sunday mornings?

Perhaps there were too many other important things going on in the Church at large for the actions of the 24th Presiding Bishop to be noticed. Perhaps it wasn't in his plan at all. No time or attention was given to the moment.

If a tree falls in the forest and no one hears it, does it make a sound?

In retrospect, it seems clear he *knew*—in a way that foreshadowed things we need to know today.

---

1. Pat Conroy, *The Prince of Tides: A Novel* (New York: Houghton Mifflin, 1986), 604.

I was covering an Executive Council meeting for the Episcopal News Service. The host diocese had pulled out all the stops, with tours of important ministry sites. Today was the day that representatives of congregations would make presentations to the Council. The first speaker represented a mission, miles away from the city where we had gathered. His talk was brief and off the cuff, as he told stories about this small group of faithful people. The applause was polite. The scope of presentations and the applause grew as we moved up the average Sunday attendance scale (ASA). When the Corporate (largest) parish's turn came, glossy three-inch notebooks filled with professional photos, pie charts, and newspaper clippings were handed out. The final speaker sat down; the Presiding Bishop thanked them all for their presentations, and then, turning to the speaker from the mission church, he asked him if he would mind answering some questions about the creative things they were doing.

There are Kodak moments that remain in the mind's eye for a lifetime, often without obvious reason. This was such a moment for me, although nothing that followed would have noted it as significant. The hosts from the corporate parish and anyone else who might have been shocked quickly covered any reaction that could have been construed as impolite. Yet the sense hung over the room: In the midst of obvious markers of success and prosperity, *this is who he lifts up as significant for leadership to hear?*

Sometimes we only see clearly through the rearview mirror.

Yet I remember there was something intangible in that room—a glimpse of something very important. It was out of the expected order of things. After all, we were meeting in one of the largest church meeting rooms in the city, and would soon be treated to an elegant reception in the very elegant parlor, which could easily hold several hundreds of people. And the Presiding Bishop of the Episcopal Church had quite deliberately chosen to highlight the contributions of the man from the smallest mission in the diocese. Images of David and Goliath. "A little child shall lead them. . . ."

Fast forward a decade or two.

In his book *Prince of Tides*, author Pat Conroy describes the sale and ultimate demise of the fictional town of Colleton, South Carolina. Buildings that were considered worthwhile were relocated to larger venues, the rest plowed under to make way for the manufacture of plutonium. The sentence that hit home could almost be considered a throwaway, caught in the end of a paragraph that leads to some pretty important action.

> "As a town, we had made the error of staying small—and there is no more unforgivable crime in America."

It's a bit like the ad on TV that asserts, "Bigger is better, right?" Our landscapes are scattered with the detritus of expendable big box buildings left behind while the out-of-town owners move on to something bigger. And downtown, the stores that once were filled with groceries, hardware, clothing, and *people* attempt to reinvent themselves as antique malls and coffee shops. A recent strip mall renovation in Lexington, Kentucky, is hailed for creating an environment where people can walk from their homes, sit down with their neighbors, and be about the business of community.

Community?

Wait just a minute! Isn't that our business—the business of the Church?

Is it possible—just possible—that as we worry and wonder about how we will have a church of the future, that a number of answers are right in our own backyards—in the small churches we've been figuratively patting on the head for years as we've moved toward and some into our own version of megachurches, with all of the corporate accoutrements?

Church-wide discussions on structure and growth tend to focus on the importance of increasing butts in the pews and bucks in the plates. Suggestions have been made on merging smaller dioceses to create larger ones, and the possibility of closing the doors of congregations that do not have an ASA of at least two hundred. Meanwhile, 2011 statistics from the Episcopal Church report that 68 percent of Episcopal congregations have an ASA of below one hundred.[2] The Hartford Institute for Religion Research reports that these suggestions come out of a cultural context where communities are being stripped of anything small: small businesses, small post offices, small schools, small downtowns.[3] The model is a model of scarcity, without consideration of the abundance to be found in small churches, as a model for part of the future of our Church, right in our own backyards.

We've been sold a bill of goods that bigger is always better—and we've come to act like we believe it, even if we don't. We've almost eliminated all of the smaller things from our world—just because they're small.

For all of the years of my life in the Church, I have given what I believed to be support to my diocese's belief in small churches. After all, we are not only a diocese of "small" churches, we are a denomination of small or "normal" sized churches. I have spent some years as a member of the Pastoral (ASA 50–150), the Program (ASA 150–300), and the Corporate or Resource (300 plus) sized congregation. It was being a part of the lives of Family (0–50) and Pastoral sized churches in my capacity as transition officer in the Diocese of Lexington that made me aware of how much I—and the Church—had to learn from them.

I recognized my unique learning laboratory while driving a road I might not ever have known, although I had lived in Kentucky all of my life. I call the epiphany moment "lessons in faithfulness from the Kingdom Come Parkway." Come travel it with me. Often it runs from small to small, in terms of neighborhoods, towns, and churches, on a landscape writ large by God. For the Kingdom Come Parkway exists, not only in Kentucky, but across the country. Certainly it goes by other names and other numbers, but wherever it exists, those roads take us away from the impersonal stretches of interstates into the personalities of unique areas of living. For all who might pay attention,

---

2. www.episcopalchurch.org/sites/default/files/downloads/domestic_fast_facts_trends_2009-2013.pdf

3. faithcommunitiestoday.org/facts-growth-2010

there are lessons to be learned that are applicable in whatever sized churches we might find ourselves—intimations of a future that is already upon us, that some people have been living quietly for generations—out of necessity. Their norm may well be one model for the church of tomorrow.

Highway 119 is an eighteen-mile stretch of primarily two-lane road that runs between Kentucky 25E in Bell County and the outskirts of Harlan, Kentucky, in Harlan County. It is also known as the Kingdom Come Parkway. For those accustomed to interstate and major highway driving, even with the occasional additional lanes for passing, the road seems narrow, winding and sometimes hilly. For those who tried to get from Pineville on 25E to Harlan or vice-versa before the mountain was cut through, this is an easy road. And, of course, there was also a time when there wasn't a four-lane 25E, or an interstate, either.

I turned onto Highway 119 on a Wednesday morning in late April, headed for an 11:00 a.m. meeting in Harlan to talk about options for transition ministry with the good folk of Christ Church. The morning sun slanted down through the lacey web of early spring trees. A hundred shades of green in as many varied shapes of budding leaves covered the hillsides, in contrast to a deep blue sky. Kentucky redbuds, whose spring blossoms are actually a brilliant magenta, seemed to glow as if they were lit from the inside, punctuating the green with breathtaking abundance.

Later that day, I would deliberately drive that road three times—reluctant to leave it behind—as if it had a message for me, in addition to its spring beauty. I have known it in the heat of summer, when the kudzu climbs, creating softly rounded sculptures encasing rusted cars, nameless bushes, and trees, and threatening to eat whatever is in its path. I have watched the fiery autumn colors punctuate the hills, and carefully navigated its icy winter path . . . always with a sense of cutting through not only the craggy mountain, but also much of what it had been easy over the years to believe is "normal" for church—and thereby, would be normal going forward.

The cut-throughs are what makes these modern roads of Eastern Kentucky possible—the black/grey walls of always moist and glistening rock where not so many years ago, through some feat of engineering, the mountains were literally sliced open to provide the possibility of such a road as 119. As my car enters a cut-through, I find myself imagining what it was like when the cut-through didn't exist; when the way in or out of an area meant travelling up the height of those massive rock walls, or around them. Each mountain was a barrier between people and parts of the state. The mountains—those beautiful, tall, rolling hills—were indeed symbols of isolation. I cannot travel these roads without marveling at the modern know-how that created a break in the pattern of isolationism. Without wondering what other barriers on what other roads in other places enforce isolation, or the residual behaviors formed by long-existent patterns of isolationism, whether geographic, attitudinal, philosophical, or theological, I travel.

The Kingdom Come Parkway takes its name both from an actual place along 119 known as "Kingdom Come" and one of the first-known million-dollar best-selling books from the 1800s, *The Little Shepherd of Kingdom Come*,[4] by Kentucky writer John Fox Jr. Fox was known for showing the contrast between the insular culture of Appalachia against a more modern "outside" world. While his romantic fiction in the local color genre is criticized today for its outdated gender stereotypes, and for popularizing an unfair depiction of the people of Appalachia, the character of the "little shepherd" (with his intense loyalty to the people who had been a part of his growing up and faithfulness to his own moral convictions) jumped into the middle of my drive-time reflections on what had become both thin place and metaphor for me.

It occurs to me that we have a similar contrast within the Church: the contrast of our smaller or "normal" sized churches

---

4. John Fox, *The Little Shepherd of Kingdom Come* (Lexington, KY: University Press of Kentucky, 1993). First published in 1903.

(one-man, one-woman shows, where the priest is sexton, pastor, and preacher) and the well-resourced program and corporate sized parishes (and the megachurches of the Protestant and nondenominational culture) where professional staffs are available to share the load. Two radically different cultures, each with their own stereotypes—and without a best-selling author to point it out!

When I hear those in decision-making roles who believe that the answer to surviving and thriving in this millennium and beyond is about numbers—butts in pews and bucks in plate—I know that they have not sat in a vestry meeting in Harlan, Kentucky, attended a community meal in Harrodsburg, Kentucky, or worked the food pantry at St. James, Prestonsburg. When I hear it said that "congregations with under 200 ASA on Sunday should be shut down," I know that the recommendations are coming from those who have not worshipped at St. Patrick's, Somerset, or St. Mary's, Middlesboro—nor in Iola, Kansas, or Alliance, Nebraska. They have not learned the lessons in faithfulness that accompany the warm hugs, the fabulous covered dishes, and the profound experience of worship at Grace Church, Florence, St. Andrew's, Lexington, St. Hubert's, Clark County or Resurrection, Jessamine County. They have not been welcomed to Calvary, Ashland, or St. Francis, Flemingsburg, or the innumerable small congregations that make up the majority of the Dioceses of the Episcopal Church.

Recently I was part of an interdenominational conference entitled "Re-Imagining Faith: For America and the World."[5] One of the discussions that emerged over the course of the two days had to do with the future of the full-time, fully compensated, pastoral ministry. While familiar with the topic in Episcopal circles, and with efforts across the Church in bi-vocational and other creative ministries, this was my first exposure to it on an interdenominational level. Seminary professors and professionals in

---

5. Held at Georgetown College, Georgetown, Kentucky, January 9–10, 2014.

the Church were matter-of-factly saying that the next generation to attend seminary needed to be prepared for bi-vocational or part-time ministry. Some participants were aghast. After all, there were scarcely enough hours in any day or days in any week for full-time ministry. How could one possibly sustain two jobs—one of them as pastor?

As I listened to the discussion, faces from small congregations kept appearing before my eyes: quietly competent leadership of Morning Prayer; the faithful visits of Lay Eucharistic Ministers to the sick and shut-in; priests managing the sacraments and pastoral care of two and sometimes three congregations; dioceses continually working to find new ways to make it possible for there to be an Episcopal presence in the hardest-to-reach areas of their cure. The heartbreaking technical fix is to let markers we have known dictate what doors we shut and what doors we keep open; where we will focus our energy. The hard work of adaptive challenges is to figure out how to harness faithfulness—the kind of faithfulness that has kept smaller churches in ministry all these years—and offer it as a proposition of the possible to a world badly in need of things that are both affordable and sustainable for the many. To recognize that we live in a culture where 32 percent of the population are self-designated "nones," with no religious affiliation,[6] and often a disdain for religion that does not live out what they espouse. In such a culture, an Episcopal presence in the small towns, villages, and neighborhoods that are home to many of these small churches, means a welcome to those who might not be welcomed anywhere else, and an opportunity to know that there are alternatives to the fundamentalism that is often rampant.

It is time to look at markers that are not the world's, and yet have the power to transform the world, if we harness them. Civility learned and practiced as normative, and thus recognized as a safe place in an unsafe world. Respect for each other—beyond

---

6. www.pewforum.org/2012/10/09/nones-on-the-rise/

size and titles. The stories and essentials of the faith that they have to offer have been collected from many parts of the country and the Episcopal Church.

As a long-time journalist and qualitative researcher, I will use the models of phenomenology and heuristics to allow the merger of stories into depictions, which represent clusters of stories revealing similar characteristics. The majority of examples in this book utilize this approach, which enables freedom on the part of the storyteller in sharing without violating the privacy of individuals. The phenomenological model combines with good, old-fashioned journalistic interviewing, in instances where individuals and locations are clearly identified.

The art of phenomenology involves systematic reflection on and study of the lived experience and consciousness of that experience of others around a specific issue, such as life in small or "normal" congregations. Heuristics is the application of qualitative research methodologies to the personal experience of the researcher, for systematic reflection on and study for the purpose of discovering similarities of the possibilities of change in the research topic. The combination of the methodologies encourages the validation of qualitative data and analysis.

The epiphany moment on the Kingdom Come Parkway led to the initial premise of this book—that the lessons in faithfulness I was privileged to learn in the small congregations of my diocese had something very important to offer the larger Church: BIG LESSONS from LITTLE PLACES which were not problems to be solved but models to study. With each interview, new threads emerged, and the always-fascinating journey of following those threads led to conversations that might have continued far beyond the agreed-upon deadline!

The end point of this study will, I hope, be an invitation to you to begin your own exploration of the BIG LESSONS in the LITTLE PLACES around you.

Truth is stranger than fiction, they say. Pat Conroy knew the truth of what he was writing about when his fictional Tom Wingo watched buildings floating down the river for relocation, *if* they were grand enough, and witnessed his own small home turned into the dust of government land because it wasn't.

Being small cannot become an unforgivable crime in the real world of our Church. It's time to stop, look, and learn; to give hope for our future.

Please join me on a journey down *the* Kingdom Come Parkway—and *your* Kingdom Come Parkway . . . wherever you find it. There are big lessons to learn from little places about faithfulness and the future.

Kay Collier McLaughlin
Lexington, Kentucky, 2014

CHAPTER ONE

"I'll Be Singing to the Cows"

*This is home because Minnie
and a few hundred other
people trust me to hold their
hands should they die. . . .*

*It is home because Angus and Minnie dared to tell me the truth. It is
home because old ladies reach out to touch our children as if they were
their own. It is home because the checker in the market calls me by my
name. It is home because I don't want to go anywhere else. What I know
now is that how this came to be home is a stranger story than I thought.
But the story usually is stranger than we first thought. . . . I know that
much that has come upon me in life I did not search out and choose,
but rather found by chance and accepted as grace. The will of God is
an intricate weaving of incidents and accidents, plans and providence.
Sometimes it works through us, sometimes in spite of us, but in all
things, it can work for good.* MICHAEL L. LINDVALL[1]

A small parish in Appalachia was probably not what Press Mc-
Cone envisioned when he completed his undergraduate degree at
Harvard, when he received his Master of Divinity degree from
Princeton Theological Seminary, or set out to serve the Presby-
terian Church. God, with an infinite sense of humor, had other
plans for Press.

Along the way, he would run into the Episcopal Church, and find
himself at The Church Divinity School of the Pacific in Berkeley,

---

1. Michael L. Lindvall, *The Good News from North Haven: A Year in the
Life of a Small Town* (New York: Crossroads Publishing, 2002).

California. It was at Berkeley that he was handed a brochure which read, "Don't let the dream of seminary die . . . come serve the people of Appalachia . . ." and subsequently found himself the Minister-in-Charge of a family sized congregation in southeastern Kentucky. After three years, Press and his wife headed west—not to the urban areas of Berkeley or Boulder—but to yoked parishes in Nebraska, eight hours from the diocesan offices. On his final Sunday in Kentucky, the son of a parishioner, holding a recent master's degree in vocal performance and planning for Met auditions in the fall, sang at the Eucharist. "I took a few lessons from Ronald," says Press, "thinking I might need to sing the liturgy at my next cure. And now, I know, I'll be singing to the cows!"

Fast forward two years. Sitting beside his study window hundreds of miles from the place he never imagined he'd call home, Press reflected with me on his life in another small town, far from urban lights. "No lines to get my driver's license, no traffic, low cost of living, lots of wonderful people. I just have to work a little harder to get to the opera!"[2]

"It's about falling in love," says Ben, a successful businessman before God called. "Once I fall in love, I'm done. Maybe in a larger place you can be defended against that vulnerability, but not when you are in this kind of intimacy."[3]

Like Press, Ben was a product of a large sponsoring church— and large expectations, both from the secular world which measured his success in dollars and corner offices, and in clergy mentors and professors who assumed a career path for him moving quickly up the ladder from a first assignment to one of "importance." "They called it 'steeple jumping' when I was in seminary," Press says. "The bigger the better. There was no sense of preparation for ministry that might not be about growing something larger; that a small church might be different in lots of ways than a large one."[4]

---

2. Telephone interview, March 24, 2014.
3. Telephone interview, March 25, 2014.
4. Telephone interview, March 24, 2014.

It was a reality Press, Ben, and others have stumbled into, as well as their love affairs with the "normal" sized" churches to which they feel a real vocation. "I want to stress the "normal," Ben says. "I am tired of hearing about "small" this and "small" that, as if the norm for Episcopal churches, or mainline churches in general, is the megachurch, or the cardinal parish, or even a good-sized program congregation. This is normal!"[5]

Church consultant Lyle E. Schaller, in *The Small Church IS Different*, states: "The normal size for a protestant congregation on the North American continent is one that has fewer than forty people at worship on the typical Sunday morning."[6] Today, too many church leaders assume that the very large congregation is the normative institutional expression of the Christian congregation. More recent data from the Duke University National Congregational Study substantiates Schaller's statistics by setting the median figure at seventy-five regular participants in worship.[7]

A number of men and women interviewed were products of small, or "normal" sized congregations. The "largest" churches experienced by this group prior to seminary were program sized, with an average Sunday attendance, according to their informal estimates, of "somewhere between one hundred fifty and two hundred" and the smallest family sized congregations of twenty-five to thirty. "I had no idea that a congregation of five or six thousand members might even exist in the Episcopal Church," says Ann, who grew up in a mission congregation in the south. "I was in my twenties, just out of college. I assumed most churches were like mine. I have always seen myself as ministering in a small parish."[8]

In 2005, the Rt. Rev. Stacy F. Sauls, then bishop of the Diocese of Lexington, looked around his diocese of predominantly

---

5. Telephone interview, March 25, 2014.
6. Lyle E. Schaller, *The Small Church IS Different* (Nashville: Abingdon, 1982), 9–10.
7. www.soc.duke.edu.natcongreg
8. Interview, June 11, 2014.

large family or small pastoral congregations and noted that for a certain number of them, the only consistency in ordained leadership was the lack of steady healthy and energetic clergy. Supply clergy to offer the sacraments were an occasional answer, as were newly ordained folks with little experience and less guidance, or folks nearing or past retirement.

"I don't think most of us answered the call to ordained ministry expecting to have to move up some ladder to be able to pay off seminary debt," Bishop Sauls said. "I think that in many hearts, there is a dream of being in a community where it is possible to be in relationships. And one thing I was becoming more and more convinced of—these parishes needed energy and excitement from their clergy, as well as vision and training."

In the Diocese of Lexington, the result was a three-year program similar to a hospital residency, in which the best and brightest are recruited from seminary graduates each year and offered a priest-in-charge position. Support systems in place aided in intentional priestly formation in the context of a "teaching parish," whose mission is about forming priests not just for themselves, but for the Church-at-large. We called this the Network, and its advertising brochure read: "Don't let the dream of seminary die. . . ."

People like Press and Ben agree—while acknowledging that it wasn't an option that anyone talked about, or considered admirable, during their years in seminary in the early 2000s. "Maybe it had to do with the economy, and the thought that as things crashed and burned, small churches were not going to be able to afford full-time clergy," says Paul, a product of those years. "The financial crash in 2008 meant that a lot of churches lost the endowments they'd depended on, and things were looking pretty bleak all the way round." Don remembers not only discouragement about the small churches, but a bleak outlook in general that suggested that indeed, his class members might be the ones to turn out the lights and close the doors on the Church in general, not just the small church. In the second decade of this millennium, there are reports from several seminaries that are looking more closely at the context of ordained ministry and what growth means, perhaps with a move toward recognition that there is value in the small or "normal" sized church.[9]

"It was OK to consider taking a small parish just out of seminary," Ben says, "but when I considered it for my second call, a trusted and well-loved mentor strongly advised me against taking the position. 'If you take it, you will die,' he said to me. I think, in retrospect, that he was saying my career opportunities would die; that I would get pegged as the guy who took broken-down parishes, and that was not a way to make a career in the Church."[10]

Bill remembers that when he gave his senior sermon at seminary, he said that he saw himself called to small churches. A seminary professor approached him afterward and said, "Why are you limiting yourself so much?" A few years into his life as a priest in a small church, a former classmate told him that he had been really frustrated with Bill because he thought he had "no ambition." "The good thing," Bill says, "was that he finally had come to see that I just loved what I was doing!"[11] The attitude of both professor and classmate seem not unusual in the stories that are told. Small congregations are where deacons and new ordinands serve—until they get a "real" church!

Phil's call to small church ministry began with his own yearning for deeper connections than he had experienced in the urban parishes in which he grew up. "I had felt isolated," he says today. "I felt connected to God, but not to people."[12] Nothing in his formal training encouraged his interest. He was encouraged to pursue further training at Oxford; he was urged to prepare to accept one of several invitations to be nominated in bishops' elections. And in the several dioceses he has served, he has continued to see new seminary graduates assigned, however briefly, to the smallest churches. As others have observed, the general understanding

---

9. Telephone interview, August 30, 2014.
10. Telephone interview, March 25, 2014.
11. Interview, May 14, 2014.
12. Interview, May 27, 2014.

is that this is the way that dues are paid, until one gets that "real" church!

Sometimes God has a funny way of getting people's attention, even when it's about falling in love. About recognizing a vocation, even if no one else does. For Press, it took a divorce that side-tracked the upward climb, and introduced him to bi-vocational or tent-maker ministry, in places where he would come to know the people of his cure in deep and special ways. Ben checked back into corporate America, where he found himself lost in a world where he once moved with the high rollers. "*This* is where I'm dying," he concluded. Something was wrong.

"So I went back and considered the calls I had rejected," he says. "Something in me had changed, had shifted. And probably something in the congregations, too. I remember something my father, who was a deacon, had said to me before I ever had the remotest idea of being a priest. He told me to look at the story of the feeding of the five thousand, which is in all four gospels. And in one of them there is a line that is easy to miss: "He sat them down in groups of fifty. He did NOT endeavor to feed them in an undifferentiated mass of five thousand people."[13]

He goes on to point out that several theories of organizational life use the number fifty as optimal for community life. "And there is the scriptural basis for those theories—as well as for the church."[14]

Bill is fond of saying that if he were in the Roman Catholic Church, he would be known as a "diocesan priest," sent by the bishop to cover congregations whose needs matched with his particular skills; congregations which often do not have the resources to conduct a full search on the open market. Serving in a similar role, but without that title, he has come to a really in-depth understanding that as a priest he is never a member of any church, but is called or sent to serve.

---

13. Telephone interview, March 25, 2014.
14. Luke 8:1–17.

Roma's pre-seminary career took place in large, urban churches, and her expectation was that she would be most comfortable in those settings. On a job interview in a rural diocese, she was amazed to discover how drawn she felt to the small parish and its smaller town than those to which she was accustomed. "I had been told that there were plenty of jobs in the Episcopal Church, but that most of them were not in what were considered prime locations, such as major cities. What I have found is a positive and sustainable way of life in an area which is an example of the kind of location where entrepreneurs are recognizing values: access to nature and recreation, lower cost of living, close relationships; and in a technological world where business headquarters can be literally any place in the world, many are choosing to locate in areas with such bonuses."[15]

Ben was correct when he noted that "something shifted." And it is just such a shift that is needed if we as a Church and a culture are to embrace not only the small or normal sized church per se, but what it represents in our value system and what it might have to offer us as we move into an uncertain future for organized religion. Pat Conroy was right when he stated that according to the values of today's culture, the mythical town of Colleton had committed the "unforgiveable crime" in America of staying small. Our culture often pathologizes "small" as an estate to be escaped from, or replaced by something larger. The marker of success is growth, without the realization that small is simply different than large, with its own characteristics and values. Check a thesaurus for synonyms for "small" and up pop adjectives like diminutive, stunted, tiny, puny, wee, runty, sawed-off, scanty, meager, sparse; verbs like decrease, contract, shrink, wane.

Karl Vaters is pastor of Cornerstone Christian Fellowship in Fountain Valley, California. He is the man behind the blog, New Small Church[16] and author of *The Grasshopper Myth: Big*

---

15. Interview, March 28, 2014.
16. newsmallchurch.com (2013)

Churches, Small Churches and the Small Thinking that Divides Us.[17] A blurb on Amazon for the Grasshopper book reads: "Ninety percent of churches in this country have less than two hundred members. What if that is not a bad thing? What if small is an advantage God wants us to use, not a problem to fix?"

Sarah was called to a curacy position when she finished seminary. Even then, she was not sure that large churches were her passion. However, she remembers being advised to "build up your pension base, and then you can follow your heart." Her heart has taken her to several "normal" sized congregations since that first assignment. For four of the five years she served "part time," she was not credited with a full year for her pension.

Just recently, she received a letter from the Church Pension Group informing her that anyone who makes a minimum of "$18,200 per year will receive a full year's credit toward his or her pension."[18] While the new ruling will not change the fact that the percentage of a part-time salary is radically lower than full time, and often what a "normal" sized church can pay a full-time rector is closer to a diocesan minimum than it is to the six figures of corporate parishes, it's a step in the right direction, according to Dr. Molly Marshall, president of Central Baptist Theological Seminary. Speaking at the January 2014 Re-Imagining conference, she told the gathering that any denomination that was sending individuals to seminary with the expectation that they will have full-time work in the Church when they graduate needs to reassess that statement, as bi-vocational and part-time clergy are the wave of the future.

Vaters states, "Yes, all healthy things grow. But growth is never as simple as *older equals taller* or *healthy equals bigger*. A pea will never be the size of a pumpkin and a rose won't reach the height

---

17. Karl Vaters, *The Grasshopper Myth: Big Churches, Small Churches and the Small Thinking that Divides Us* (Fountain Valley, CA: New Small Church, 2013).

18. Changes to Church Pension Fund Retirement Plans PDF aa86e41e7d9 51355383b.cb342165bfeaa4f2927aec8e5d7cle41f.r23.cf2.rackcd.com/pdf

of a redwood no matter how much you water them, fertilize them, or teach them redwood growth principles. It's just not in their nature. All healthy, living things reach their optimal size at maturity, then they grow in different ways from that point on. What if that principle applied to churches? I have come to believe it does. If the Church is one body with many parts, isn't it possible, even likely, that the Body of Christ needs churches of all sizes?"[19]

And exactly what *is* a small church? According to Carl Dudley, although the majority of churches are small, the majority of people belong to larger congregations.[20]

And those small protestant churches, he writes, are "everywhere." "Small churches are found in every kind of community—city, suburb, and rural village; they are rich and poor and they exist in every kind of cultural background. The rural small church is the unmoved image of serenity in the midst of mobile America: in summer, the crossroads church under the spreading tree; and in winter, the heart of the Christmas season, surrounded by driven snow and issuing a warm "Season's Greetings!" Small churches are equally ubiquitous in the urban areas. Including the storefront churches with their many tongues and languages, small churches embrace more people in the congested cities than in the scattered witness of our rural areas. Even in affluent suburban neighborhoods, small churches can be found. They are the young congregations that never grew. They are the small intentional fellowships, issue-oriented, and without walls. Small churches have taken root everywhere."[21]

It sounds so simple.

But the shift, the turnaround, demands that we as a culture as well as a Church begin to respect the dignity of each entity as well as each individual, and come to know it for who and what it is. We can then begin to learn from it, as well as to expect others to

---

19. Vaters, *The Grasshopper Myth*, 6.
20. Carl S. Dudley, *Making the Small Church Effective* (Nashville: Abingdon Press, 1984), 11.
21. *Ibid.*, 21.

teach how to minister in such an environment in our seminaries and training.

We cannot teach what we do not know, nor have experienced. And many of the representative samples with whom I spoke were clear about their preparation for ministry—and lack of preparation for the uniqueness of the small church, or the validity of a vocation in ministry where growth is not the measure of success. There were exceptions: those who were educated alongside Licensed Local Pastors with an emphasis on knowing that they would likely be serving places without associate, organist, choirmaster, or secretary; a priest who had experienced a course entitled "Practical Ministry," taught by lecturers who were themselves active in parish ministry.

Responses to this model reaffirmed the benefit of both the academic and practical sides of ministry, not just theory. Several clergy indicated that their knowledge of small churches came in a field education parish during seminary. The most structured example was of an "Issues in Ministry" class in which they were asked to do social analysis and case studies on a variety of types of congregations, from the declining urban to the burgeoning suburban and the rural, with a goal of determining what was actually possible for each.

Tony, a senior cleric who has seen the Church from staff positions in its seminaries, as well as the largest to smallest of its churches, joins his concern with seminary graduates of several institutions and ages. "We are in the business of mis-training," he states. "There are those places preparing students to chant Evensong in Cathedral environments who will serve parishes with congregations of five. Others are preparing students for the *avant garde*—politically, liturgically, and socially—which is never going to fly in some of the neighborhoods and small towns. And others are so busy in-fighting and worrying about survival, not to mention how to provide a good, solid nonresidential experience to offer ordained leadership to congregations, that they can't possibly focus on the formation of priests!"[22]

---

22. Interview, May 12, 2014.

One of the characteristics of the small church, says Schaller, is stability or plateau in size. "The continued existence of larger congregations requires the sustained efforts of many people to keep that water running uphill. . . . By contrast, most small congregations tend to stay on the same plateau in size, year after year, decade after decade, just as the water tends to find its own level. It is not uncommon to see large congregations shrink in size, but it is unusual for the long-established congregation, averaging thirty, forty, or fifty at worship, to double or triple in size."[23]

The call to a ministry in small or normal sized congregations is real—just as the call to a larger congregation can be real. It's not that one is right and one is wrong. They are different, and they have different things to offer different people.

Carl Dudley writes, "In a big world, the small church has remained intimate. In a fast world, the small church has remained steady. In an expensive world, the small church has remained plain. In a complex world, the small church has remained simple. In a rational world, the small church has retained feelings. In a mobile world, the small church has been an anchor. In an anonymous world, the small church calls us by name."[24]

Like most love affairs, the call to vocation, clerical or lay, in the small church is not without its own issues. Families of all sizes have their bumps and scrapes, and the system that is the small church is no exception. Vaters says, "We need to be careful that in valuing small churches, we don't devalue what big churches bring to the Body of Christ. Every type and size of church has problems. And each of them brings something of value, too."[25]

And what of training for a vocation to small churches? Not an awareness of the problems that need fixing so a small church can function like a large church, but a recognition of the unique nature and characteristics of the small church as a set of givens.

---

23. Schaller, *The Small Church IS Different*, 12
24. Dudley, *Making the Small Church Effective*, 17.
25. Vaters, *The Grasshopper Myth*, 57

With exploration of what some of these characteristics mean, as opposed to how they are wrong, and how they might have value not only for their own congregations, but for the organized Church in general. And certainly, for looking toward the Church of tomorrow.

The Rt. Rev. Mike Milliken, bishop of Western Kansas, is the only bishop currently serving simultaneously as rector of a congregation and bishop of an adjudicatory of twenty-eight congregations, only four of which are parishes with compensated, full-time clergy. Perhaps uniquely prepared to serve in this situation, Milliken received his Master of Divinity degree from the Episcopal Theological Seminary in Kentucky (ETSKy, now defunct) where he recalls being taught by professors who emphasized that there are lots of little churches but no insignificant ones. "The message was always kept in front of us," he says, "that you don't base intrinsic value on size."[26] It's a message and experience that travels with him today.

In retrospect, it appears that the Rt. Rev. William R. Moody, third Bishop of Lexington, might have been on track when he revived ETSKy in an effort to supply the small congregations of his diocese with trained clergy. Often criticized for his conservative positions on the ordination of women and other movements in the Church, his efforts to provide theological education for married students, students who needed to work while attending school, and even some who might not have completed college might be viewed from today's perspective as envisioning a need that most in his time found unacceptable for the Episcopal Church. Perhaps he was speaking to the truth of today's Church and world.

Jack, a small church product himself, recalls a seminary class in empowering congregations. "The professor had served in several small dioceses which had more small than large congregations, and thus was clear with us that this—small or "normal"

---

26. Telephone interview, September 11, 2014.

sized congregations—*is* the church. And rather than try to focus on megachurches, which we are *not*, we need to focus on the gifts small churches bring."[27]

For every Bishop Mike, Jack, and professor with small church experience and appreciation, there are the stories of the Presses, Bens, Sarahs, and Romas who are in ministry in "normal" sized parishes today. It's important to heed what they are telling us:

- Many seminaries are, by and large, teaching out of the experience of a 1950s' forward corporate model with a one-sized modality that sees "normal" as numerical growth toward a program and resource model, and the "small" parish is a problem to be "fixed" by church growth strategies or brought to a death.

- The "career" trajectory is the expectation of upward mobility in full-time service to the Church where the best compensated years receive the highest percentage of pension contributions.

- Vocation to a different trajectory is not encouraged, prepared for, or monetarily rewarded.

- The majority of resources that concern small churches are based on a large church/numerical growth model and do not understand or appreciate unique aspects of smallness which may have important cultural and spiritual learnings.

Several astute voices add that the bias and lack of understanding goes deeper than seminary training or professional ministry, to the question of what *is* the right size to do what we do as a church? What is sustainable in each situation? And how do we know once we've reached sustainability when big enough is just big enough?

---

27. Interview, September 13, 2014.

Lesson on faithfulness #1

God's most important call might not be up the ladder of congregational size.

For discussion

"Here I am, Lord; is it I, Lord?
I have heard you calling in the night
I will go, Lord, if you lead me
I will hold your people in my heart."

- **For personal reflection:** Have you ever had a call you thought might be from God, which went against your own and others' plans and projections for your life? How did that feel? What did you do?

- **For group reflection:** How do you experience the culture and the Church's attitude impacting the life of small churches around you? Attitudes toward "smallness"?

- **For action:** What action might you consider taking regarding what you learned in this chapter?

CHAPTER TWO

From "So Far Away" to "Part of the Family"

A proper community,
we should remember,
also, is a commonwealth.
A place, a resource,
an economy. . . .

It answers the needs, practical as well as social and spiritual, of its
members—among them, the need to need one another. **WENDELL BERRY**[1]

"Why are you paying so much attention to us all of a sudden?" the Senior Warden queried, the obvious distrust written across his face and resonating in his voice.

"Because you're part of the diocesan family, no matter how far away," the transition officer answered, aware that the man had a right to his question, and the diocese had to own it. Providing a sacramental presence a couple of times a month with hopes that nothing too serious would come up before the bishop's annual visitation had been all we and they could hope for over many years. And all of a sudden, here we were with this big idea, suddenly traveling however many hours it took to get there and back, offering a different kind of support and attention than they had known before.

---

1. Wendell Berry, *The Art of the Commonplace: The Agrarian Essays of Wendell Berry* (Berkeley, CA: Counterpoint Press, 2002), 63.

In most dioceses, time and dollars go only so far, and building on the awarenesses revealed in Chapter One, most were doing the best they had been trained to do: stretching time and resources, endeavoring to teach "normal" sized parishes how to function like big parishes, and wondering about the resistance. Depending on the size of the diocese and distance from diocesan headquarters, the number of part-time and supply clergy available—well, in short, even those dioceses that professed a love of and interest in small churches deserved that senior warden's question.

Small churches were a problem to be solved, over and over again in Lexington. The majority of answers had to do with sending newly minted clergy out to do the best that they could do—or finding someone ready for a quieter life toward the end of their career. It was a survival model at best.

This is not an area where technical fixes were or are going to change things. The way we've thought about small churches has not gotten the job done. This is an area where there is a willingness to look at the adaptive challenges; to admit we don't know the answers and that it requires our most creative, out-of-the-box thinking as well as the best and brightest of our human resources. It will also take a rethinking of how we compensate clergy and how pensions are calculated. In terms of attitude and retirement income, the tail has been wagging the dog. The reality of the Church in the twenty-first century (and beyond) demands that we pay a different kind of attention.

Part of the adaptive challenge for judicatories and all denominational leadership, including seminaries, is to assume an attitude of learner rather than teacher when it comes to the small or normal churches. What might be learned if these congregations are viewed as normative? What ah-ha's might emerge if existing models for church growth, congregational development, and other aspects of life in the institutional church were set aside and the small church was approached with the open mind of seeker, researcher, inquirer? What if we were to discover that our institutional practices don't fit all sizes, and that there might be a better way to assign resources?

More importantly, what might happen if institutional attitudes toward small churches changed from cost efficiency in a time when endowments and budgets are diminishing at best, and non-existent at worst, from problem focused to possibility focused? And in those instances when, after real vision is translated into real creative efforts, there are some churches that will die, the Church became intentional in naming and dealing with the fear, and then the grief, that accompany these deaths?

"My diocese gives lip service to caring about small churches," says Tony, a senior cleric, who has served the Church in congregations of several thousand, as a seminary professor, and as both interim and supply. "And then I experience a diocesan officer come into a small congregation and with a coldness that feels mean spirited, tell them it's time to 'face the music,' and prepare that they will be closed. The behaviors don't live up to the vision of valuing small churches."[2]

In another diocese, a member of the vestry recalls such a "conversation" with a diocesan official. "We don't need someone to help us to 'face the music,' or tell us that closing the doors is inevitable," she says. "Why can't they give us some help? We need a regular priest, not a priest d'jour, who offers us nothing in the way of continuity or relationships. One of the last ones who came here didn't even prepare a sermon, telling us that we didn't 'need' a sermon, that way we would 'get out faster.' As if speed dating was what it was all about."[3]

Harriet has her eyes wide open—to the lack of youth and young families, the aging of church members, the exhaustion of the congregation—and the lack of vision and energy from the diocesan office. "I told them, 'Honey, we're not ready to shut these doors. You can go on home!'" She smiles ruefully, "I imagine that woman went back to the diocesan office and said 'You won't believe the crazy person I ran into at St. M's!' As far as I'm concerned, they're the ones who are crazy. They have no idea what life is like

---

2. Interview, May 12, 2014.
3. Telephone interview, June 5, 2014.

in this part of the state and diocese. They don't know our history. They don't understand that when they sell this church, they are selling our family histories. They are selling the ashes of our ancestors, and our children, buried in the columbarium. Have they asked any of us to be a part of a new vision? Do they know what might work here?"[4]

Experienced hands like Tony name this disconnect between small churches and the judicatory. "They feel completely disrespected and uncared for," Tony says sadly. "And I have to say they're right on target. In those places where all efforts fail, and closure *is* inevitable, it's time for intentionality in dealing with the fear, the anticipatory grief, and the searing grief of actual death of their beloved church. Instead, the fear and the grief are allowed to turn into cynicism and distrust of the diocese, which plays out as sarcasm and anger."[5]

In the Diocese of Maine, Bishop Stephen Lane is vividly aware of small churches, which comprise fifty-five of his sixty congregations. His four canons on a recently reconfigured small staff join him in life "on the road," a way of being in and with each congregation on a regular basis. He believes that conversations about what God is calling people to do in these congregations have to start a year or two in advance of crisis time. "Unfortunately," he says, "most diocesan offices are strapped, and sometimes, despite best intentions, we don't pay attention until someone screams bloody murder. In order for us to be present in our parishes, we have to figure out what things we used to do that now need to be let go—there's not time or energy for it all."[6]

Lane's meetings to consider God's call and the possibility of different ways of doing church have led to several experiments that could well be models for others in the Church. In Mars Hill, St. Ann's was home to an aging congregation of five. The building was sold for community use, the agency that purchased it taking

---

4. Telephone interview, June 5, 2014.
5. Telephone interview, June 5, 2014.
6. Telephone interview, June 10, 2014.

over the ministry that St. Ann's had once provided. Members of St. Ann's joined a neighboring congregation, whose members also continue the ministry—a slightly different Episcopal presence, a slightly different identity.

Five congregations in another area of the Diocese are in conversation about the possibility of shared mission and ministry, and are presently worshipping together once a month. They have been "in holy conversation" for over a year. At a recent all-day meeting, Bishop Lane shared that they moved "from despair to hope and are beginning to talk about 'what ifs.'"

Only one church in the Diocese of Maine has an assistant, and that parish, St. Alban in Cape Elizabeth, has entered into an agreement with St. Peter's in Portland. The assistant is three-quarters time at St. Alban and one-quarter time at St. Peter's; she lives in the rectory directly across the street from the church and is supervised in her work by a priest from Trinity, Portland. It's a "complicated" arrangement, says the bishop. Along with having an in-residence priest at St. Peter's for the first time in many years, suburban St. Alban has become more invested in city ministries and has begun to host monthly meetings of area clergy for mutual support. "These are wonderful, unintended by-products," the bishop acknowledged.

Bar Harbor and Southwest Harbor have been sharing a priest in an arrangement soon to enter its third year. In cold and wintry Maine, people can be scarcer than money—and offer a taste of cultural, geographic, and distance factors that are a huge part of the small church riddle.

"This is slow, developmental work," Bishop Lane says. "It takes a lot of time. But we don't have another choice. We have to be present, even if it is to witness the death of what we have known; to remember together, to grieve, and then to be open to opportunities God has for us. This is what death and resurrection is about."[7]

Ann, Rona, and Zack are aware that the myriad of materials that come to them regarding stewardship, formation, youth, and

---

7. Telephone interview, June 5, 2014.

other aspects of parish life, both programmatically and administratively, are "created for the benefit of the larger parish." "There are few, if any, places to turn for help for small churches . . . just the assumption that all of this fits every size church, and that there are enough hands in the office to handle it all."[8]

Ralph is also beginning to wonder about all of the great ideas and programs that get put into practice as normative for the system. "All good things," he acknowledges, "without any way to assist churches with compliance." Recalling pastoral congregations with whom he has been associated, he speaks of volunteer treasurers who come in to sign checks on their day off; folks who try their best with local resources to deal with the business and administrative tasks required. "It's hard to load all of this on the backs of small churches, one-person shows, *and* expect them to do mission and ministry, too."

"It's a little like a book I've been reading, not on church, but colonialism," he says. "Viewed from the long distance, it's easy to see places as states, while from the inside, people know them differently, as places they live, with distinct characteristics that sometimes are not recognized from the outside. It's like creating a program about raising crops for a country we know little about. They've been raising crops for generations, even if we think they're doing it the wrong way. Sometimes there are reasons that programs don't work."

He sighs.

"It's like we've forgotten about the social analysis, the community organizing, the learning that needs to happen before we march into something. Better is better—bigger is not better everywhere. But we have to be able to do the hard preliminary work—not just go in to put out fires."[9]

Bishops and senior clerics agree that we as an institution are suffering badly from a long-held professional clergy model. It's not a bad thing to be well trained, have high standards and

8. Telephone interview, June 5, 2014.
9. Telephone interview, June 10, 2014.

professional skills and competencies, but notions about "career track" are a detriment to both church and clergy. It seems clear that there was once a "social contract"—an implicit agreement that a person who took on the burden of the cost of seminary had a promise of lifelong employment, respect and position in a community, and a comfortable retirement. That contract is no longer valid. It has been broken.

Only 30 percent of Episcopal clergy today are full time.[10]

Bishop Lane remembers well the days of moving from seminary to curacy in a large church, and in his own case, to a next position as a one-man show in a pastoral sized parish.

His remembering is tinged with chagrin.

"I've never worked harder than as rector of that small congregation," he says. "I was the 'everything.' I had a volunteer treasurer, a part-time secretary, and a part-time sexton. I had not been trained how to train others to teach, or how to lead. It was by-the-seat-of-my-pants stuff, out of necessity. It just wasn't possible for me to do it all. I remember going on vacation that first year and knowing I was worn to a nub. I have never been as exhausted in my life!"[11]

Ann describes a typical day of ministry as the rector of a pastoral sized congregation. "It began with a run to the cancer hospital in the city (about forty-five minutes away), with travel and wait time interspersed with texts and e-mails about parish matters, coffee and pastoral conversation with a college student. It's three o'clock before I ever get to the office, and there's a vestry meeting tonight. My accountability is to the people I care for here—not to staff meetings and complex programs." She pauses. "I'd like to find resources that really support me, in the way of mentoring, resources, spiritual direction; in terms of how I can take care of myself in this kind of spiritual ministry, how I can live out my vocation, how to develop a rule of life and a plan that 'gets it.'"[12]

---

10. www.cpg.org
11. Telephone interview, June 5, 2014.
12. Telephone interview, June 11, 2014.

Lesson on faithfulness #2

The institution has been complicit in the small church struggle, and is only beginning to own its lack of awareness of the importance of such ministry.

For discussion

"Because of an apple, Eden fell and Troy was destroyed."
−Marty Rubin[13]

- **For personal reflection:** Have you ever attended a "small church" (under one hundred people average Sunday attendance) for regular services? If you are a member of a "small" church, have you ever attended a "large" church for regular services? What was your experience?

- **For group reflection:** How do you experience your diocese or judicatory attending to the smaller churches in your area? What impact does that have?

- **For action:** What action might you consider to learn more about smaller churches?

---

13. www.goodreads.com/author/quotes/1936218.Marty_Rubin?page=10

CHAPTER THREE

Recognizing Faithfulness Upside Down

*It's never making a
move without consulting
your values, and then
sticking to them heart
and soul. . . .*

*More difficult still, leading by values requires successful managers to set
aside their pride as masters of their domain and turn themselves into
servants of their ideals and values. Managing upside down is not just a
job: it's a vocation.* **TOM CHAPPELL, CEO OF TOM'S OF MAINE**[1]

The instructions had been very clear. There would be a vestry
meeting with the bishop's representative to go over the terms of
a letter of agreement and make plans. Seated at the table was the
Transition Officer of the diocese and elected members of the vestry of St. L's. Around the periphery of the room, men and women
were filling up the chairs.

The first time it happened, I was confused. I thought maybe
I had not made my instructions clear. But no, I was to continue
learning. There was no confusion. Whatever is important enough
for the vestry to know about is of concern to the rest of the
church. "It's our church and we care about it" was an attitude I
began to recognize. While it might be an area for education—that

---

1. Tom Chappell, *Managing Upside Down: The Seven Intentions of Values-
Centered Leadership* (New York: William Morrow, 1999). Pg. 5

in the Episcopal Church, the vestry does, indeed, represent the congregation that elected them—how many bigger institutions would not like to have the invitation to the congregation, that vestry meetings are open, accepted on a regular basis by most of the congregation, simply because they care?

"Visiting small or normal sized parishes with a church growth mindset, carrying a briefcase of institutional theories is a little like going into a foreign country and electing to stay in American hotels and eat American food. One is likely to miss the experience of uniqueness and return home comparing it all to the good old USA, with the "different" context coming up short every time!

It takes time; time to *be* in the communities of not one but numerous small churches to recognize the particular cultures, to enjoy each uniqueness and to begin to be aware of dimensions of faith that might be easy to miss without this immersion. In other words, what might seem normative to judicatory offices and larger churches might have a different norm in smaller churches.

In institutional mindset and lingo, it's a little like entering a foreign country and being unable to read the signage or speak the language.

It's a bit of managing upside down, as Tom Chappell, founder and CEO of *Tom's of Maine*, writes in his book of the same name. He brought to his company a concept of "Values-Centered" leadership, based on "Seven Intentions," which include:

• Connecting your own self-interest to the greater good

• Knowing who you are and what you value

• Seeking advice from others

• Venturing out into new areas

(Prepare for heresy.) How do you know who you are and what you value? This is **not** something that can be dictated from the top of a pyramid, but must be accessed from within the body, the community, itself. In Episcopal circles, who we are and what we value as a part of a worldwide communion is one thing; how that is lived out and expressed in a local community and faith fellowship is quite another. That can only be accessed from the inside out.

Curiously, or perhaps not so curiously (here comes another heresy), some of the most lively, stable, and healthy small churches encountered during this research were independent or congregationalist in nature, each responsible for their own lives. While we teach that the diocese is the central unit of the church, and congregations of all shapes and sizes join together under this umbrella for strength and support, in these days of economic downturn, the opposite appears to be true.

The organizational entity on which the strength of the enterprise rests has its energy focused on the program and resource sized parishes as most economically feasible, with many small churches seen as expendable, or way down the priority list in assigning line items and staff support. "Managing Upside Down" is a partnership—a bit of a heresy in "Hierarchical Episcopalese," which, like most businesses, is a pyramid, with power residing at the top. Says Chappell:

> "In managing upside down, power flows in the opposite direction—from the market, customers, and employees. In a values-driven company, innovation can come from anywhere; indeed, the main responsibility of a values-driven leader is to encourage new ideas to come from everywhere. 'Superiors' and 'Subordinates' have no place in the creative process. The muses of creativity do not care about job titles. Two heads (or more) are always better than one. The wisdom of the group trumps the opinion of one individual. In a values-oriented company, a leader's primary job is not to wield power, but to draw it from every member of the community."[2]

Exploring resources about small churches, I discovered that the majority of published or online publications had a problem-focused view of small churches: this is how we "fix" them and grow them. Interestingly enough, by the time we finish fixing and

---

2. *Ibid.*, 19.

growing, they are no longer small or normal sized churches, but program sized churches!

Both experience and research indicate that the jump from pastoral to program sized parish is the most difficult to make and to sustain—with numerous examples of congregations that have "reached" program status, only to "fall back" to pastoral status. This has been viewed as a problem to be fixed: resistance to growth. But perhaps there could be other reasons?

What if we flip the whole thing upside down? We **begin** with the assumption that there is something unique about small churches that has kept them alive with a reasonable stability these many years, and that within that uniqueness there are lessons that can benefit the whole.

In the Tom's of Maine sense, the small churches here are the market, the customers, the employees, the ones whose *day-to-day* and *year-to-year experience* in the small churches holds some information that is untapped as a resource for the future of the Church. It is information that is impossible to see from the tired old pyramid. We must (get ready for still another heresy) *flip the pyramid and be intentional about learning what it contains!*

The Upside-Down World of the Small Church

One of the most important characteristics of the "normal" or "small" church is that of **belonging**, one of the basic human needs according to psychologist Abraham Maslow's hierarchy of needs[3]— the sense of ownership that leads to an intense caring. In a consumer-minded culture, membership in a small church is not about being served and moving on if the product isn't what is desired; it is about serving something foundational in people's lives. In some rural or isolated areas, there is only one Episcopal church for several hundred miles. In more populated areas where there might be choices available, there are people who are intentional about seeking out a church home where they will know members of the community.

---

3. www.learning-theories.com/maslows-hierarchy-of-needs.html

"I'm not sure if ownership is the word I'm looking for, or if it is a sense of pride, but my experience of it has something to do with what I call 'magic,'" says Ann, rector of a pastoral sized congregation in the southeast. "Now, I know it's not magic. But say I walk through the garden on my way to the office and I notice that the lawn needs mowing. Of course, I forget it the minute I open the office door, but lo and behold, later that day or the next day, miraculously, there is someone out there mowing. It's their church, like their own home, and they are going to attend to it."[4]

While the flip side of ownership and caring can be over-investment and over-functioning that lead to under-functioning and burnout (as well as some other unpleasant things!), this aspect of the small church is worth considering with new eyes.

As the new priest-in-charge at St. Saviour, Roma brought a background in nonprofit management with her brand-new ordained status. Seeing the potential rather than a problem in the "ownership" practices of her flock that led to meetings of the "committee of the whole," she offered a quick teaching on effective organizational behavior, lifting up the "committee of the whole" practices and adding some practical thoughts that made sense to her people. "I told them this was something that happened in small organizations everywhere," she says, "and that one of my concerns is that it's easy to get burned out working this way, if you're not careful."

The folks of St. Saviour had experienced burnout more than once in their corporate lives, and they were more than willing to see what suggestions Roma brought with her for strengthening their life together. "Once they got the idea that some of the things they (the vestry) were spending hours on (plus anyone else who happened to come to the meeting) could be handled by committee, and reported to the vestry, things started to operate more effectively. Meetings were shorter and accomplished more."[5]

---

4. Telephone interview, June 11, 2014.
5. Interview, March 28, 2014.

Caitlin had served on the vestry of her small parish several times and had assumed that "committee of the whole" scenario was a given, just as taking your turn on the vestry was. "We were so small that it didn't seem to make any sense to have committees." St. Mary's was without a priest—again. As luck (or the Holy Spirit) would have it, Father Rick, an experienced retired priest in the diocese, was available to spend several months with the parish. "They are unique in many ways, as each parish is," he says, reflecting on his experiences with St. Mary's. "But in another sense, their image of themselves as too small to have good, healthy practices of organization bogged them down into these long, drawn-out meetings that everyone dreaded. In that sense, I treated them exactly like I did every parish I served. We looked at what areas needed committees, and got them appointed. As they did their work and reported back to the vestry—and often, that 'committee of the whole'—more things got done, and people stopped dreading meetings."[6]

"But, it was clear to me that they were there because they *cared*. It mattered to them what was happening. That's a priceless commodity!"

Less Formal Approach to Finances

Jay, a transition officer, spoke of his first experience with a small church vestry. "The budget that they showed me didn't seem to tell the whole story. As I would ask how something was paid for, the answer was always, 'Oh, we take care of that when it's needed.' I had little or no experience with small churches, and this went against the grain of everything I knew about stewardship. So, I went to a priest friend who had spent most of his working life in small churches, and he told me this was not unusual."[7]

One theory about finances and the small church is that a mentality of fear drives the way finances are handled. If all of the

---

6. Interview, September 8, 2014.
7. Interview, September 9, 2014.

funds are in the hands of the church, and the judicatory makes a decision to close that particular congregation, what is to happen to the funds?

For some this is certainly true. However, taking a longer look with Karl Vader's comments in mind . . .

Redwood growth hormones don't always work for roses.

Could it be possible that rather than attempting to squeeze every aspect of the small church square peg into the institution's round hole, we might step back and study a few of the norms of congregational life in the small church in order to discern patterns that are effective in certain size entities?

In his book *The Small Church IS Different!*,[8] Lyle Schaller talks about the difficulty lay persons (who come to small churches from large church lay leadership positions) and clergy (who have been trained in a one-size-fits-all-church finance model) have seeing that there are positives for the small churches in their less formal and systematic approach to finances.

"When they understand the need, our people will respond," is the assurance given by thousands of lay ministers every year to recently arrived and worried ministers who envision financial calamity only a few months away.[9]

"It's a both/and kind of thing, I believe," says Martha, who served several small congregations in her diocese. "On the one hand, there is the most amazing generosity I have ever seen. The air conditioner breaks, and another one appears. No questions. On the other hand, the lack of understanding that someone's generosity is paying more to mow the grass each month than they pay the priest has not been thought out in terms of what it means to the overall health of the parish."[10]

Schaller continues, "One reason the small congregations are so tough (in contrast to the institutional fragility of the typical huge congregation) is that the members do rally around and respond

---

8. Schaller, *The Small Church IS Different!*, 30.
9. *Ibid.*, 18.
10. Interview, February 12, 2014.

to a clear and visible need. While the per-member giving level of the typical small member church is lower than in the typical large congregation, the dependability of the people responding in a time of need is one of the distinctive characteristics of the small congregation."[11]

Stewardship folk inevitably respond with concern about developing a theology of giving, a spiritual discipline of giving that gives out of gratitude to God, rather than in response to a particular need.

What if—what *if*—there *is* a lived theology of giving behind this response, as surely as an articulated theology of giving? What if the very dependability is part and parcel of the spiritual discipline of giving? Is it possible that this question has never been asked; or has an assumption been made that *all* people in *every sized church* need the identical theology and discipline?

Involvement of Laity and Appreciation of Clergy

Perhaps second to the upside-down characteristic of informal stewardship is the importance of the role of the laity paralleled with huge appreciation for clergy. Many small churches have periods of part-time clergy in their institutional memory. If the church was to remain active, it was up to the laity to make it so. "We have a healthy respect for those 'magic hands' that preside over the Eucharist and Holy Baptism, that perform weddings and funerals," says Jim, whose multiple roles in his small church include junior warden, senior warden, Sunday school teacher, vestry member, lay reader, and lay Eucharistic minister, "and we are so very grateful when we do have clergy with us on a regular basis. But we don't stop when we don't have clergy, either full or part time. We need the church and each other too much for that."[12]

---

11. Schaller, *The Small Church IS Different!*, 18.
12. Telephone interview, April 5, 2014.

Incorporation into Leadership

Another upside-down theory in small churches regards incorporating members into leadership roles. At a recent diocesan council meeting, members were asked to reflect on how their spiritual journey led them to this leadership role in the diocese. "I had only been in the church a year when I was asked to run for the vestry," a member said. It was a statement repeated numerous times among the members. In small churches, new members who are regular in attendance will soon find themselves drafted into further service, where in the majority of program or corporate parishes, earning a leadership role might take several years and more than one run for the vestry before one is elected! While family ties are also a factor (the expectation that each generation of a particular family will produce at least one leader to fill the role that their parents and grandparents once filled), new members are incorporated quickly, with the expectation that the job will help them grow in their faith formation and their commitment to the church. While large churches wonder about how to incorporate members into their complex systems, to arrive at a small church is to become part of it.

Communication in Community

Get ready for yet another heresy. Call it grapevines or call it triangling or gossip, the fear is the same. And it is real and valid. Gossip and innuendo can, in fact, be very, very harmful. But if knowing and being known are indeed hallmarks of a smaller church, the word-of-mouth sharing of information is a part of that "knowingness." The grapevine is a given in most small churches—and if it is not already a good, healthy grapevine, it can quickly become that in order to use the practice of the "tribe" for effective communication. Word-of-mouth connects small congregations: who is sick, who is pregnant, who is in the hospital, who just got engaged, whose child was accepted to college, etc., etc. In a larger setting, word-of-mouth functions something like the old game of "I'm going to pack my suitcase . . ." with participants seated in a circle and whispering in each other's ears. By the time the last person receives the message, it generally bears little relation to what was whispered the first time! With fewer people, it's hard to garble the message too much. If there's a mistake, someone is sure to correct it. Newcomers may be on guard for signs of unhealthy triangulation; however, this can be a prime example of positive triangulation.

Policies That Don't Fit

Institutional time frames may call for some compromise with life in the small parish, as well as the adjustment of some processes. In most dioceses, there are norms regarding membership on vestries that would preclude more than one member of a family serving at a given time. When a congregation is composed of four or five extended families, the existence of a bishop's committee or vestry may be dependent upon the service of several members of a family. Obviously, issues of control and healthy behaviors need to be understood, with intentionality toward effective operations and healthy human interaction.

As Phillip stated, "There are times that rules are meant to be broken. The Bible is a love story, not a book of rules and regulations. We are in danger of losing a whole part of the story when we focus on the rules and regulations."[13]

As noted earlier, congregational development specialists have long taught that the most difficult leap in growth comes from the pastoral sized parish to the program sized parish. There are many examples of parishes that reach the numerical status that would indicate they have moved into the program category, only to fall back to pastoral in size—again and again.

This phenomenon has been viewed as a problem to be fixed. After all, more butts in the pew means more bucks in the plate, as well as a change in styles of both ordained and lay leadership, and ministry opportunities offered.

---

13. Interview, April 4, 2014.

But *what if* there are legitimately those churches whose *set point*—whose DNA, as well as whose geographic setting—finds their operating level as a small or normal sized church, whose life appears to manage upside down, by institutional standards?

Set point theory comes from a health care model that looks at internal regulatory controls that dictate how much body fat and weight one has. According to the set point theory, some individuals have a high setting, meaning that they tend to have a naturally higher weight as a set point, and others have a low set point and therefore a naturally lower body weight.

The set point theory suggests that despite dieting efforts, the body tends to return to its set point weight, although regular, consistent exercise may adjust the set point. Some refer to the set point theory as the internal thermostat. Set point theory is valid in other areas of life as well, and psychologists have been studying it in such areas as life happiness and well-being. A dictionary definition for set point is as follows: an internal regulatory system for maintaining a relatively stable physiological condition in the face of changing external circumstances, as body temperature in a varying climate.[14]

Perhaps there is a "set point" in the life of the church—one we have been endeavoring mightily to adjust. Perhaps there are those congregations whose set point is higher, and those whose set point is lower. Both may be "norms" in our institutional life.

On the website of a small parish in Vermont, these words encapsulate the healthy small church, managing upside down by the big-church church-growth "rule book"—and offering lessons in faithfulness for congregations of any size:

> St. L's is an intentional Christian Community deepening faith and broadening love.
>
> We are a diverse group of followers of the Way on a journey of discovery to seek just what it means to be disciples of Jesus Christ in the twenty-first century. To this end, we seek to be a community where God's gift of hospitality, of welcome and love,

---

14. www.dictionary-reference.com/browse/setpoint

is freely given to all and any, within, and beyond, St. L's. We seek to be a community where a joyful levity is cultivated, made known, and for all weighed down by the loss and gravity of life. We seek to be a community where unity in diversity exists; where us replaces them; and connections replace divisions. Above all, we seek to be a community where trust in God, and of each other, replaces fear; where, with the Spirit's unfailing help, we are raised above our own limitations, and those boxes of our own or others' creation. We invite you to observe our journey through this website. Better yet, if possible, join us on this journey as followers of the Way in this our time. Come and see.

In Christ's love.[15]

Lesson on faithfulness #3

Upside down is a perspective that is dependent on where you're standing. There's a unique faithfulness in practice that deserves a second look.

For discussion

"The Book of Acts tells the story of a handful of men and women who by the grace of the Holy Spirit did not leave the world the same way they found it." –www.Jesus.com

- **For personal reflection:** Have you ever experienced a truth that was "upside down" from what you had been taught/believed? How did it come to you? What difference did it make to you? What did it change?

- **For group reflection:** How is it different to think of the small church as a "leader" and "teacher" rather than a "problem" to be fixed or someone in need of being shown how to do things the right way? How might it change your relationships with others?

- **For action:** What one step can you take to learn from small churches?

---

15. Signage at St. Luke's Episcopal Church in Chester, Vermont.

CHAPTER FOUR
Bigger Than You Think

Bible—66 books
Individual—40 books
People groups—13 books
Small churches—8 books
Numbers—1 book
KARL VATERS[1]

St. Mary's, Middlesboro sits in a southeast corner of the state, where Virginia, Tennessee, and Kentucky come together. During the walkabouts for candidates to serve this part of the state, newspapers from three states were placed on the informational table in the parish hall, demonstrating the geographic area that members of the congregation call home. For part of the congregation, Knoxville provides the closest medical center and big-time shopping; for others, Virginia, and for still others, Lexington, Kentucky. It's natural to think of church as something bigger than this church when its small, white clapboard building is a container for folks from three states! It is also bigger than the average Sunday attendance or other statistics noted on their parochial report. More bishops are beginning to ask their congregations to report on how many souls are touched by the church in a given week—whether or not they ever sit in the pew on Sunday morning, become a pledging member, or serve on the vestry!

In a western suburb, a small congregation sits in the middle of a neighborhood that has been gentrified. The newcomers to

---

1. Vaters, *The Grasshopper Myth*, 119.

the area are not particularly comfortable with the neighborhood or church old-timers who are definitely not comfortable with them! Yet incorporating the neighborhood as part of the church's mission seems crucial to its viability. An art gallery sits near the church. And has become the scene of an alternative worship service, led by the parish. The liturgy is more an approachable Morning Prayer than the Eucharist to this community. Activities are intended to integrate the new, and the old include small groups and non-Eucharistic agape meals, as well as one-on-one time.

St. Francis in Russell Springs, Western Kansas, literally forty miles from the nearest gas station and surrounded by cattle ranches and wheat farms, is served by a circuit-riding priest with three other congregations for which he is responsible. And it is the sponsor of camp Run-a-Muck, a summer opportunity for inner city children to experience a working cattle ranch. A faithful, loving extension of the Kingdom.

There's The Church of the Upper Room, also in Western Kansas. Every Sunday morning, a group of twenty to twenty-five people gather in their priest's house at ten o'clock for Bible study, eleven o'clock for worship, and lunch for everyone at noon. It is a true community of Anglos, Hispanics, Episcopalians, and otherwise. The top pledger is a shepherd—yes, one who daily tends the wooly type of sheep—who is eighteen years old.

Bigger Than You Think

"That 'bigger than you think' is about far more than geography," says Bishop Milliken. "We need to get some people past identifying with church buildings." While acknowledging the history and sentiment connected with structures, he continues, "There is this idea that dioceses have unlimited dollars to help keep buildings afloat and clergy in place. I had to tell this to a congregation recently, that if that is what they are counting on, they just won't *be* anymore. And if they quit, I will sell the building, invest in a storefront with an altar at one end, a coffee pot at the other and a day care in the middle, and we'll have one service in English and one in Spanish. We have got to reimagine what the church looks like—and it *is bigger* than any picture we have had before."[2]

A priest reports attending a church growth seminar, "I asked the presenter how they recommended funding a new church plant. A loan from the diocese of around two million dollars was suggested. That would be about ten years worth of our diocesan budget!"[3] Moving on to the next topic, he asked where the church looks to plant new congregations. The response was on the growing edge of metropolitan areas with an over 50,000 population.

"Not much help if you're in a diocese where your largest city is 40,000," mused the cleric, wondering if perhaps the vision about church development was too small, when the possibilities are bigger than one might think—just different.

Lesson on faithfulness #4

Growing the Kingdom by touching souls is more important than ASA.

For discussion

"For the love of God is broader than the measure of man's mind."

- **For personal reflection:** When have you been touched by an expression of church that made you aware of the breadth and depth of the Kingdom?

- **For group reflection:** Can you think of a time that your local congregation experienced this awareness?

- **For action:** How might you facilitate your own and your congregation's experience of "bigger than you think"?

---

2. Telephone interview, September 11, 2014.
3. Interview, May 14, 2014.

CHAPTER FIVE

Miss Bessie, Pleasant Company, and Part-Timers

*The world of small church
people is built of people
and relationships. . . .*
ANTHONY G. PAPPAS[1]

Every small congregation must have a "Miss Bessie." Maybe her name isn't really Bessie.

Maybe it's Sally. Or Mabel, or Susanna. Whatever the name, she has been at the organ or piano for more years than many parishioners have lived. She has outlived many children of the parish. Her eyes are fading, and it's hard for her to see the notes in the hymnal. But giving her talent to support the ministry of music in the congregation has been her gift to God for most of her life—in this particular place. She may know that it's harder and harder to sit through a service, but what would she do without it? And how is the congregation going to work around the heart and soul of this faithful servant?

There are also those congregations where there isn't even a Miss Bessie, only an electronic servant programmed to play particular service music and some favorite hymns. And there is Pleasant Company, the group of local musicians who have become

1. Anthony G. Pappas, *Entering the World of the Small Church* (Washington, DC: Alban Institute, 1988).

part and parcel of St. Patrick's, Somerset, with their hammered dulcimer, fiddle, flute, and other folk instruments. "Glory to the Father; Glory be to the Son; Glory be to the Spirit, All glory to our God!" The exclamation points cannot really express the spirit of the singing at St. Pat's. After a recent service, a nonagenarian exclaimed, "I love our chamber group!"

Faithfulness is music, lifted to God in whatever way it is possible.

"We got to church a little early on Maundy Thursday to practice a duet for that night," says Joslyn. "As we walked in the front door, the priest and organist were heading out the back door, both looking a little shaky. The organist was having what they thought was an anxiety attack. They needed to go to the emergency room and have her checked out for sure. My duet partner volunteered to drive so the priest could continue with preparations for the service. The priest looked at me and said, 'Joslyn, will you play?' Of course, I said yes. He knew I could play the piano, and I knew he didn't expect me to play the organ. I've been playing hymns on the piano since I was a little kid. I'm not a professional, but it was OK. We had a quick Plan B and the service happened, without too much disruption." It wasn't what anyone had planned, or expected. It wasn't especially fine from a musical perspective. But it was very real, intimate, and heartfelt.[2]

Plan B did not have an assistant waiting in the wings, nor was the backup expected to sound like a usual Sunday. It wasn't really about the sound. It was about the community singing together for the service, and praying for the organist (and probably for the "sub" as well!).

At St. Barnabas, the small electronic organ's name is "Dora." Once upon a time there WAS a Dora, who was the "organist." She had not grown up in the Episcopal tradition, so the chants and other service music were tough for her to understand. Luckily, the keyboard at the church had a recording element where music could be stored and retrieved as needed. Long after Miss Dora had retired, the "Dora" still had recorded service music in

---

2. Interview, February 24, 2014.

its innards that could be accessed by the push of a button, lovingly taped by an accomplished friend of Miss Dora. The old recordings are getting a bit scratchy, so these days, whenever there is a chance to get a fresh version from a musical visitor or friend, "Dora" gets an update! These days, Dora is getting a more regular workout from an adult parishioner who is taking piano lessons, and developing an unusual agility for a beginner. Dora and Bud share duties, with Bud assuming more and more of the responsibility for accompanying congregational singing as his repertoire grows. The people of St. Barnabas are enthusiastic cheerleaders for their "new" musician, celebrating each new hymn added to his list and encouraging him every step of the way.

There are extraordinary talents that sometimes have a regular place in the pews of even the smallest churches, and not always as the professional. "I teach music all day, every day," says Kaitlin. "I am always the one organizing and leading. At church, I just want to worship, which includes singing, but I have no need to be in charge. This is simply my gift to God—and a language between us."[3]

Louise's soaring soprano is sought after throughout the region. On Sunday, it fills the small sanctuary at St. P's, and encourages others to sing out as well. Tom is a professional baritone who comes back to his childhood church as often as possible, happy to offer special music.

And there are the children. At St. Paul's, they're called the "JOY!" ministry, just the pure joy of children learning how it feels to sing praise, as well as how to sing. There are the children of St. J's who learned "The Irish Blessing" to sing as a special farewell gift when Father F. retired. It might not have been musical perfection; it was perfection of the hearts of the ones who gave and the one who received. There were the three kings on Epiphany Sunday at Church of the Advent, ages seven, eight, and ten.

At Christ Chapel, there are often more singers with aging voices in the choir stalls than worshippers in the pews. Congregants

---

3. Interview, February 23, 2014.

come in quietly and take their seats while the choir is processing (for those who still can process) to the first hymn. And there is St. L's and St. T's, where guitar players are constantly learning new chords, enlarging their repertoires to include music of the liturgy and hymns from the hymnal—a work always in progress. There are congregations experimenting with "paperless music,"[4] an approach to music and community building that is sung as a call and response.

There are Episcopal praise ensembles in place like St. M's, where a guitar, keyboard, and several "upfront" voices (who happen to be present that day) lead the congregational singing. Guitars provide an accompaniment in numerous small congregations, with a parishioner playing the chords with more or less skill. There are upright pianos that have seen better days in family homes before being "donated" to a congregation, some who have a regular keyboardist and other instruments that sit idle except for periods when a teenager or other volunteer fills in.

Dale arrived as the new rector at St. Mary's to discover not one but two organists who had been a part of the life of the parish for several decades. Friends since high school, they had become estranged over the years and no longer spoke to each other. Age and physical disabilities had made a difficult decision worse. What to do?

At St. Mary's, the new rector needed a new position description for the music director who was resistant to his expectations. Dale was clear about his canonical duties regarding music. Rather than acquiesce to the norm as it was explained, the music director decided to retire, leaving only one organist for the parish. He was suffering from degenerative disease, which was severely impacting his feet and legs and his ability to keep a tempo, which resulted in inability to accompany the singing.

In conversation, it became clear that he was aware of his limitations, but had a deep desire to reach his fiftieth year of service to the congregation, which was fast approaching. A proficient

---

4. www.allsaintscompany.org/resource/how-lead-paperless-music

volunteer musician from the parish stepped up to accompany the singing, while the organist concentrated on preludes and postludes. The parish was able to celebrate his fiftieth anniversary and to provide a "good goodbye" honoring his work over the years.

While small organizations all too often can fall into less-than-businesslike practices, and overpersonalize situations, the intimacy of the smaller entity can also encourage humane and relational solutions to personnel issues, but not without good business practices and healthy solutions in mind!

Music programs are not the only personnel areas to consider in small churches. One of the traps of church growth theory is the encouragement of churches to function like a program church in terms of staff—with the subsequent danger of the intimacy issue taking a dramatic turn for the worse. Often part-time secretaries, parish administrators, Christian Formation, and youth workers as well as musicians come from within the parish. Casual, informal arrangements seem to work well—and then, when things go wrong or there is not enough money in the budget to sustain the position, a relationship with a member is compromised.

For those trained in the church growth model, attendance on the cusp of the pastoral/program transition (ASA 150) means moving toward more than part-time help. Church growth theorists encourage the movement as a positive step toward the goal of growth.

Often, the move includes a youth worker and Christian Formation person and a part-time sexton. There is a flip side to such advance planning, however. More than one small parish representative interviewed lamented the situation in which they found themselves when the job transfers of several pledging units meant a drop in resources available for even part-time salaries. There is a great reluctance to make adjustments when members of their community are involved and personal stories known. The smaller the membership, the greater impact of the loss of just one pledging unit on the house of cards, which just might come tumbling down in terms of paid staff.

"My wife was the volunteer youth director for many years," says one vestry member. "And I'm not sure that year after year we have enough young people to warrant a paid position. But somewhere out there seems to be the idea that if we have a paid person, we will grow."[5] All too often this kind of thinking pushes a parish to hire a part-time person without checking local demographics to observe in relation to theory. If a community is growing, the effort and finances required may be worth the price; if the community is stagnant, or dying, there is little chance to have constant influx of new people.

A priest adds, thoughtfully, "I am just beginning to even consider the idea that a small church might be the size it is meant to be for its context, and that numerical growth isn't the only measure of growth or valid ministry. Coming out of a corporate background as well as the church growth model of seminary training, it's a whole new way of thinking."

"But it makes me wonder if this is why the huge resistance we've been taught about when a church is on the cusp of moving from pastoral to program. It's always been taught that there's something *wrong* with the church that resists. What if it knows its own best size, and the answer is to continue to build on the real caring of the members that is a gift of the small church, and not try to stretch into a model that we cannot afford? Does that stress to pay salaries increase ministry? Does it really touch more souls for Christ?"[6]

Lesson on faithfulness #5

Making a joyful noise to the Lord, and other aspects of parish life, might look different in the small church.

For discussion

"Oh Jesus I have promised, to serve Thee to the end."

---

5. Interview, August 28, 2014.
6. Telephone interview, August 30, 2014.

- **For personal reflection:** What roles do music and liturgy play for you in worship? What jobs would you personally be willing to do to keep your parish alive and well?

- **For group reflection:** "By the book," what size is your church and is it functioning effectively for its size?

- **For action:** What steps can I/we take for functioning that fits our size and our budget?

CHAPTER SIX

Gathering Around the Table

Bread. Wine. A dinner table.
The firm clasp of hands as
we say grace. The warm
flame of candles. It is all an
affirmation of incarnation,
of being versus non-being.
MADELEINE L'ENGLE[1]

There's the Table (God's), and there's the table. The kind where people gather for regular meals. The one that the community knows about. Somehow, it seems that the smaller the church, the larger the table. Take the one at St. Philip's, Harrodsburg: the last Friday night of each month there's a Community Meal, with a Capital C. People in this little town have come to count on it. When it first started, it fed about thirty. Now it regularly feeds up to ninety. And then there are the tables at Christ Church, Harlan. Once a year, the congregation brings all of their best linens and silver, china, and crystal to the undercroft of the church. They sell about eighty tickets, personally cook the most elaborate meal you could imagine, and then auction off stuff to the same people who bought the tickets. All of this is to make money for a worthy cause they have chosen in the diocese or community. Last year they raised eight thousand dollars in one night for the community

---

1. Madeline L'Engle, *The Irrational Season* (New York: Crosswicks, Ltd., 1977), 212.

57

medical center. There aren't hundreds of hands to do the work at either place. Just the faithful people who show up Sunday after Sunday and workday after workday to be sure that not only are the doors staying open, but they are being God's face and hands and feet in the world.

Faithfulness.

There's Pot Luck Sunday at St. John's, Corbin, where men and women from the homeless shelter are asked to join the congregation for Sunday dinner. In an article entitled "In Praise of Small Churches," Joan Huyser-Honig writes, "The small church worships and eats together," pointing out that when church size is measured by human relationships such as those developed over meals with the inclusion of children in an intergenerational manner, "the small church is the largest expression of Christian faith."[2]

Food, says the Rev. Peter Doddema, rector of St. Philip's, is the work of his congregation. It is a catalyst. "We move by food," he offers.[3] Certainly the Community Meal is the most public manifestation of his statement. It has been transformational for this small, historic parish in a town of eight thousand. St. Philip's might at one time have been considered the "peculiar little church" in this area of Mercer County, but the end of the month feeding program has changed all of that.

"We have two kinds of guests," says Doddema, "those who need a healthy meal and those whose living circumstances cause an isolation that welcomes the companionship as well as the food of the gathering."[4]

Little by little, folks around town began to be involved. A check here, a volunteer there. Today, the Methodists supplement the end-of-the-month Community Meal with a mid-month offering. The Disciples take their van around town to see that those in need of transportation have a way to get to the church. "It's

2. Joan Huyser-Honig, *In Praise of Small Churches*, worship.calvin.edu/resources/resource-library/in-praise-of-small-churches/
3. Telephone interview, August 30, 2014.
4. Telephone interview, August 30, 2014.

wonderful to watch them assisting the people with disabilities, welcoming every person,"[5] Doddema says enthusiastically.

And he is clear that a huge learning has been the difference between outreach and evangelism. "I think that there was an expectation when they first began that the Community Meal would translate to more people in the pews. A real learning for everyone has been that if the Community Meal does not result in new members per se, but in souls touched for the sake of the Kingdom, it is OK."

Doddema is equally clear that Christ's Table extends itself in other ways in his life and the life of the congregation. "If the Finance Chair wants to talk, frequently it's over coffee or lunch. My Ministry Support Team meets over lunch. I enjoy meals with people in their homes, in restaurants. I find that food helps people relax, the conversation flow."

At St. D's in the southeast, single adults often gather at the coffee pot after the eleven o'clock service as a departure point for a weekly lunch to which "everyone is welcome." "Sometimes there are seven or eight or even ten of us; sometimes just one or two, but it's a great way to welcome new people and a favorite way to spend what is often a lonely time for folks," says one of the "lunch bunch."[6]

At St. J's, the "lunch bunch" is an eclectic group that changes in numbers and configuration each Sunday. Sometimes the group goes Mexican; sometimes it's an all-you-can-eat buffet. "It really doesn't matter where we go," says Rona, "just that everyone knows they are welcome. It's an extension of the centrality of the Eucharistic feast in the life of this place. It's also important that there is always someone or more pitching in extra so that no one is left out because they can't afford it."[7]

At a small congregation in a small town in the southeastern United States, the faithful of Ascension had a checkered history

---

5. Telephone interview, August 30, 2014.
6. Interview, March 28, 2014.
7. Telephone interview, September 10, 2014.

of stable ordained leadership. In love with their liturgy, and grateful when supply clergy made the Eucharistic celebration possible, they also worried that others in their small town thought them "odd" and that natural attrition would eventually see them fade away. Through the determined efforts of a committed bishop, staff, and the willingness of the parish to venture together, a priest who was able to offer part-time service and his own gritty determination and love of small churches came into the picture. During Lent, the parish offered a "sacred meal" to the community-at-large.

"We broke bread together, and then we had some readings and discussion. Then we had dessert. And then we had wine. It might not have been orthodox in form, but it was truly a sacred meal. The community of Ascension felt well fed, and there were some people there who had never darkened the door of an Episcopal church before."

"There are some people who might call it a way to increase numbers. I call it a way to offer food for the soul to all who are hungry. The focus makes a difference."[8]

At St. John's in Parsons, Kansas, members were aware that there was no campus ministry and there were no Episcopal students at the nearby community college. However, they decided to reach out by going to a nearby laundromat on Sunday evenings and offering "Latte and Laundry." Equipped with their own coffee machines, volunteers provide coffee and conversation while the laundry is being done. At the beginning of the semester they hand out bags of school supplies, assembled as a get-acquainted gesture. On their birthdays, students get a free load of laundry and a birthday card. At Thanksgiving, the church provides dinner for the football team and any students who remain on campus. Their guest list includes residents of a nearby fixed-income apartment building, youth from the local youth crisis center, and church members. St. John's average Sunday attendance is thirty-two.

---

8. Telephone interview, September 10, 2014.

At St. Paul's, Clay Center, the ministry around food started innocently, with an awareness of the manager of the public swimming pool, who just happened to be the sister of a church member. She noticed that the pool was serving as an unofficial afternoon day care during its noon to 8:00 p.m. summer hours, with kids dropped off as their parents headed for work. Many, she noted, had not eaten lunch and would have no dinner. The church decided to offer hot dogs, one day a week. One day morphed into two. Tacos were added as an additional menu item. Soon St. Paul's was recognized by the Department of Parks as an official summer lunch site and received grants from the city and the local ministerial alliance. Kitchen equipment was upgraded. A registered dietician from the parish now plans the meals. The program has been so successful, it has been replicated in two other locations. The average attendance at St. Paul's: thirty-eight.

Recently, NPR's "On Point" featured the story of a small Presbyterian Church in the Blue Ridge Mountains that had closed its doors in 2012, and like most empty buildings, was slowly disintegrating. That is until Edwin Lacey came along. A musician who felt the call to seminary in his late thirties, he knew that when his denomination saw a church's numbers in severe decline, the property was often sold.

Lacey thought the area might be open to a different use of the old one-room church. He and a friend poured sweat equity into the building and opened in May with about a dozen congregants. They called it the Wild Goose Church.

For Lacey, the name fits his quest to build a new congregation in a remote area in the day of declining church attendance, in a building and an area where a church had failed. The symbol of the wild goose is important to him. "In Celtic Christianity, the symbol for the Holy Spirit is a wild goose, rather than a dove, because they feel it's more powerful and wilder, and there's a little sense of humor with it. And a wild goose will come up and bite you right in the seat of the pants, exactly like the Holy Spirit will."[9]

---

9. "On Point" NPR Interview with Wild Goose Church, May 25, 2014.

More than twice the original dozen are now drawn to the weekday evening service, where rocking chairs in a circle replace pews, and a fireplace centers where an altar might have been. Folks arrive from around the area, the majority neither Presbyterians or claiming any other denomination. They come bringing crockpots of food, eating utensils, banjos, guitars, fiddles, and other Appalachian instruments. They rock, they eat, they sing, they read scripture—and they discuss.

"Just because I have a seminary education does not mean I know as much about scripture and theology as some of the people in the group," says Lacey. It's about participation. About community.

And it's about gathering around the table, with wine in mason jars. Excessively different, someone said. Perhaps. But perhaps one does not need any descriptor except the words of one of the favorite songs from the Wild Goose Church:

I'm gonna eat at the welcome table
I'm gonna eat at the welcome table—alleluia
I'm gonna eat at the welcome table
I'm gonna eat at the welcome table—alleluia!

I'm gonna eat and drink with my Jesus
I'm gonna eat and drink with my Jesus—alleluia!
I'm gonna eat and drink with my Jesus
I'm gonna eat and drink with my Jesus—alleluia!

I'm gonna join with sisters and brothers
I'm gonna join with sisters and brothers—alleluia
I'm gonna join with sisters and brothers
I'm gonna join with sisters and brothers—alleluia!

Here all the world will find a welcome
Here all the world will find a welcome—alleluia
Here all the world will find a welcome
Here all the world will find a welcome—alleluia![10]

---

10. Lyrics by Dan Zane, www.songlyrics.com

Lesson on faithfulness #6

We've treasure to give away—no matter our size or location . . .
and often it happens around a table—an extension of THE Table.

For discussion

"I'm gonna eat at the welcome table."

- **For personal reflection:** When have you experienced a sacred meal outside of the Eucharist? What happened? How does the Eucharist "feed" you?

- **For group reflection:** How does your church "feed" others?

- **For action:** How might I/we become more involved with feeding souls who are hungry?

CHAPTER SEVEN

Westward, the Women— North, South, and East, Too!

*Talitha cum, I heard. I hear
it still. When I'm frightened
and unsure, feeling smaller
than a woman, I hear the
voice telling me, Talitha cum.*

RUTH LAWSON KIRK[1]

It was shortly after the first women were ordained in the Episcopal Church. A long-time Disciples of Christ minister was engaging in some good-natured chiding of her Anglican cohorts for our come-lately position on the timeline of women's ordination. She declared that the Disciples got a head start because women were the only ones willing to board the trains bound for the western frontier, and face the unknowns that would confront them as they pioneered for God, so they had to be ordained in order to get on that train.

Whether the story is apocryphal or not, its sequel plays out today in small towns and churches across the country. Perhaps there aren't literal trains to board to reach the destination of a parish, but aspects of pioneering are as true in the north, south, and east as they ever were in the westward movement.

---

1. Lindsay Hardin Freeman, ed., "Talitha Cum, Little Girl, Get Up," in *Wisdom Found: Stories of Women Transfigured by Faith* (Cincinnati, OH: Forward Movement, 2011).

Exactly what does this have to do with small churches and faithfulness?

There are two true statements about women and small churches. In general, there are more women willing to consider a small church assignment than men—in order to *have* a parish; to *be* a rector and answer God's call. While there are many small congregations that are happy to have an ordained woman—there are also communities where a "lady preacher" is pioneering in relationships—with other clergy, with the community at large.

Cindy is the only female in the ministerial association. "You mean you all have a LA-A-ADY preacher?" they said when Cindy first came. The good people of The Church of the Ascension never turned a hair. "We sure do!" they replied cheerfully. And they just kept on doing what they've always done—and a lot more. One of Mother Cindy's favorite things is the Girls' Club—the regular meeting with teenage girls who have been put in a hopefully supportive environment because of difficulties they have had at home, at school, or even with the law. The fact that Cindy is female is a great plus for the girls of the Girls' Club. She is a gift of faithfulness to the needs of a small community.

Extroverted Rona arrived in Culver ready to hit the ground running. Each day she would walk downtown and introduce herself to the various businesses and community agencies. Naturally, she wore the collar that clearly announced that she is a priest. There was a bit of confusion over what they should call her: Mother? Sister? Ms.? After the initial confusion, people in the community began to recognize the big smile and friendly greeting.

Then came the day she decided to visit St. H's nursing home, run by the Roman Catholic diocese. Rona entered the door wearing her collar and friendly smile. The lady at the welcome desk smiled, and then stuttered a bit. Who in the world was this *woman* in a clerical collar?

Graciousness, a non-anxious presence, and perseverance mark the Cindys and Ronas of the church. It would be easy to think that women's lib had erased all bias regarding female clergy as we inch toward a complete breaking of the glass ceiling with a potential for female president.

Just as the Disciples of Christ women pioneered westward, hardy, determined pioneers winning the hearts and minds of the north, south, and east as well with their commitment to God and the small churches and communities in which they are called to serve, women continue to pioneer in churches today, often facing gender discrimination within the small communities where congregations welcome the ministry and lives of women in ministry.

Lindy was snubbed when she arrived in Portnum. She called around to get information about the ministerial association (no one had called to welcome her!) and showed up for the monthly meeting. The greetings were chilly, at best. The meeting was short, and no one asked her to go to lunch afterward. It was a scenario that would repeat itself for many months. Lindy continued to attend. She ignored the snubs. When the community Good Friday service plans were announced in the local paper, her name was not on the list of those who were serving in some capacity.

She attended as a member of the congregation, sitting with members of her parish, while other ordained folks were on the platform or serving in some capacity. It might have continued in that manner for a very long time. Or perhaps Lindy finally would have become tired of being the polite one, and confronted her colleagues, the six male pastors who made up the association. Or, she could have ignored the whole thing, because Labor Day is not exactly on the liturgical calendar.

But in Portnum, the annual Labor Day Prayer Service was a big deal. And the pastor of the largest congregation in town always headed it up, handed out parts, and played host at his church. The day before, there was a fire at the big church. The sanctuary was badly damaged, and the pastor was hospitalized with smoke inhalation. It appeared that the noonday service on Labor Day might have to be cancelled. The rest of the ministerial association seemed paralyzed. No one but Pastor Jones had ever handled this event.

Lindy made a couple of calls, asking if the members of the association would be willing to meet at the McDonald's to see what they might do. She listened to the grief that hung over the group and the town. She heard the stories about other prayer services, and what they meant to people.

And finally she said, "Could I help? We'd be glad to have it at St. F's. We could divide up the things that Pastor Jones always did, and have special prayers for him and his church. You all tell me what needs to be done, and I'll get a few of our leaders and make it happen."

Lindy remembers that no one looked her in the eye. She didn't care. She was just glad they had come to McDonald's, glad they had sat down and told their stories. Glad when one by one they slowly began talking about what they were willing to do and accepted the invitation to hold the prayer service at St. F's. Things changed after that. Maybe it was simply time, Lindy says. For sure it was a God thing. She couldn't have stayed the course without an explosion or two all by herself. No one would have wished for the fire, of course. But, God *can* use all things for good. Pastor Jones was truly appreciative and came by to tell the lady priest he was grateful when he got out of the hospital. Several more years down the road, it's hard to believe that Lindy hasn't been a leader in this group all along.

Women have been pioneering in places that might not be known as new frontiers, but live that way. Mimi was asked by her bishop to go to a small congregation that had been served by the same nonstipendiary priest for over thirty years. As his retirement from both the workforce and the church loomed, fear was rampant. How could the church possibly survive? He was what they knew as the Episcopal Church.

Several of the congregants had an idea. There was an ordained man in town who was not serving a congregation of his denomination, and often came to St. J's, wearing a clerical collar, and expressing an interest in becoming an Episcopalian. Surely he would be a quick and easy answer to this dilemma!

Ecclesiastical hurdles remained, of course—and no one knew whether or not the young man (who, by the way, had a nice young wife and several young children, so most certainly, he would attract a new generation of worshippers to the aging congregation) had any interest in jumping those hurdles. In the meantime, Mimi was willing and able to travel to the parish on a weekly basis. She faced a congregation that could easily have been construed as a classroom facing a substitute teacher when the beloved home-room leader had been sidelined. Not only was she *not* their long-term leader, she was a *female*!

Mimi, like Rona, Cindy, and Lindy, has her own sources of support with whom she can vent about what it feels like to be a talented female in a male-dominated system (still). And like Rona, Cindy, and Lindy, Mimi keeps on keeping on. Low key. Faithful to the familiar service. Smiling at the announcements and coffee hour. Sharing stories of her own growing up as an Episcopalian in another state.

This time, the community rallied first. Mimi was quickly invited to lead a prayer at a community gathering. Then to preach. It wasn't long before the community of St. T's was preening a bit as folks downtown talked about their wonderful "preacher." Mimi's warm smile and firm but gentle guidance into diocesan life are meeting more and more warm smiles in return, every Sunday. A few of the folks who didn't get their way with the bishop are choosing to stay away—for now. Mimi is not concerned. She inquires about them and hopes they'll be back.

Lesson on faithfulness #7

Joining the past and the future are part of the ongoing call of the church in communities large and small.

For discussion

"One more step along the world I go; one more step along the world I go
From the old I travel to the new; keep me traveling along with you.

*Round the corner of the world I turn; More and more about the
world I learn*
All the new things that I see; you'll be traveling along with me.

*As I travel through the bad and good; keep me traveling the way
I should*
Where I see no way to go; you'll be telling me the way I know

*Give me courage when the world is rough; Keep me loving when
the world is tough*
Leap and sing in all I do; keep me traveling along with you

*You are older than the world can be; you are younger than the
life in me*
Ever old and ever new; keep me traveling along with you!"[2]

- **For personal reflection:** What other biases and isms are still a part of your life? Had you noticed this bias?

- **For group reflection:** Why does this bias exist? Where have you experienced examples of it?

- **For action:** What might I do to change this practice?

---

2. Text by Sydney Carter. Copyright by Stainer and Bell, Ltd (Admin. Hope Publishing Company, Carol Stream, Il 60188). All rights reserved. Used by permission. www.oremus.org/hymnal/

CHAPTER EIGHT

Being Present

There are a lot of things big churches can do that Small Churches can't do. . . . There are also some great things that Small Churches can do that big churches can't.

KARL VATERS[1]

It's a little A-frame building tucked back in a hard-to-find neighborhood in a college town at the gateway to Appalachia. Morehead, which started out as a state teachers' college, is now a university, with a pre-med program, a musical theater program, and a space science major. What the Episcopalians do is a little strange to the students, many of whom hale from Appalachia—although a few faculty have over the years found their way to the doors and became active members. But the gift of St. Alban's is a presence that says, "The Episcopal Church welcomes YOU"—and means it—no matter who you are. Men and women, including young people who might not find a welcome anywhere else in the places they came from or this gateway community, can find a place in the A-frame building where the Body and Blood of Christ are offered freely, and the word of God is about love and acceptance.

Hunter is nineteen. He is deeply in love with his bi-racial high school sweetheart. His parents are not happy with Hunter and

---

1. Vaters, *The Grasshopper Myth*, 67.

refuse to recognize Brianna. Neither Hunter nor his parents are regular churchgoers, although they are officially members of the tiny Episcopal Church in their community where Hunter's grandmother is one of the leaders in the congregation. While they're not in the pews every Sunday, Hunter and Brianna know that they have a welcoming "family" at St. J's. The people there not only welcome them when they come to services, they care about these young people's lives. How are college applications going for Brianna? Does she need anything for prom? How is Hunter's job going?

Hope Moravian Church in New Jersey has twenty regular members, give or take a few. These twenty members annually offer a summer country adventure camp for disadvantaged and challenged kids from surrounding urban areas; city kids enjoying life in a small village and the farmland around it. Jack, a seminarian, was assigned to the congregation to assist with the summer program. Shortly after his arrival, the pastor resigned, and Jack became the worship leader as well as the summer assistant.

"I had never been a part of a small worshipping community," Jack says. "I grew up in an urban church that was pretty large, and have experienced other larger churches. But the faithfulness of this group and the huge impact they have on that community and area really made a huge impression on me about what presence means, and what a small church can do."[2]

In the Diocese of Kansas, only eight of the forty-two congregations have an average Sunday attendance of over one hundred fifty. Thirteen have an ASA below thirty. But an Episcopal presence is strongly felt in places like Iola, where there is a community college. The cross country coach was chatting with a friend who is a member of St. Timothy's Episcopal Church. He wondered how in the world he was going to feed his team when they arrived on campus before the food service opened for the semester? The friend thought that perhaps St. Timothy's (ASA 23) might be able to help for those few days, and that they did.

---

2. Interview, September 9, 2014.

Around Christmas time, the basketball coach told the cross country coach that he had no idea how he was going to feed the men's and women's teams who would be on campus for practice before school opened in January. "There's this Episcopal Church . . . maybe they can help you, too."

St. Timothy's has a mission for feeding hungry people. Their freezer is always stocked with casseroles for those who might need them. This might have been a slightly larger challenge, but St. Timothy's fed fifty athletes for three weeks. Records show, for example:

Six 9 x 13 pans of casseroles
40 pounds of ham
6 pounds of pasta
30 pounds of peeled potatoes

More than a dozen of the parish members were involved in making the rib-sticking food. There were take-out containers, fruit, granola bars, and cookies. Many of the team members had come from the inner cities of faraway states and had never tasted pork loin, or turkey and mashed potatoes and gravy. The grateful team members assisted in cleanup, packed snack backpacks for children for weekend nourishment, ate with the kids, and often went to their ballgames and other activities. Real relationships. Real presence.

In the Wichita area, a church with an average Sunday attendance of twenty meets in a storefront, where they are the ongoing supplier of clothing through a weekly giveaway. If they were not there, their absence would surely be felt, says a spokesperson. Their presence is making a difference. Another small congregation with an ASA of thirteen offers tutoring for elementary school students. A member who is a banker teaches financial literacy classes.

St. Peter's in Paris, Kentucky, has a Sacred Arts presence in the community. The newly renovated parish hall of the historic church offers gallery space, and a performance and meeting venue. The church is open for community Gallery Hops, as well as Advent Musicals and lunches open to the public.

There's a move afoot to extend the arts presence in the most remote areas of the Diocese of Lexington, beginning with the traveling collection from the Cathedral Gallery which would be displayed in the sanctuaries of each small church, welcoming those who might never feel comfortable attending a worship service there. The art shows will be precursors to opportunities for EfM-type Bible study, where people are offered an opportunity to experience a different approach to scripture.

Presence.

Lessons on faithfulness #8

Relationships: presence, invitation, welcome, and intentional inclusion matter

For discussion

"The greatest gift you can give (yourself or anyone else) is just being present." –Rasheed Ogunlaru[3]

- **For personal reflection:** Have you ever been in an environment where you were unable to be yourself? How did it feel? Where did you go to feel safe?

- **For group reflection:** In what ways is your church a true presence in your community for those who might not be accepted in other churches?

- **For action:** What can you do to increase your church's presence in your community?

---

3. www.goodreads.com/quotes

CHAPTER NINE

What Does It Take to Be the Church?

*You see, everybody is searching
for something of value, but
so many of us don't know
what it is, and we don't even
know that everybody else
is looking for the same thing.*

ROBERT B HORINE[1]

People are fond of saying that all a small church can do is try to pay its bills and maintain a mostly outdated and too-big structure in order to serve the few people that show up on Sunday morning. The only metric that counts is bucks in the plate and butts in the pews . . . and something called "church growth." The thing I've noticed about faithfulness is that while people care about their buildings, and tend them with as much care as they give their children, the thing that keeps the doors open is the sense of faithfulness that is committed to giving away whatever treasure they have, and caring for each other and their community. It may not be about "church growth" in terms of numbers, but about growing the church in terms of souls. I think of the grocery program at Church of the Advent in Cynthiana. The food pantry at St. James, Prestonsburg. The quilting group at Ascension, Mount

---

1. Robert Horine, "Raymond," in *January Court* (Lexington, KY: St. Michael's Press, 1983).

Sterling, which supplies bedding for St. Agnes' House, a hospitality ministry.

A few years back, there was a motel on the outskirts of Frenchburg; when the vicar and his wife would drive by, they would notice that a group of Hispanic folk were clustered just outside one of the unit doors. After observing this for several weeks, the vicar made a few inquiries and learned that there were at least a dozen people, possibly more, calling this one room "home." It was early summer, and the vicar began to think about the increasing temperatures. His church was small, but there was an undercroft that was air-conditioned, and had a TV and a cooking unit. What if the church could reach out to this family and offer them some temporary housing until they could get their feet on the ground?

He presented his idea at a parish meeting. The first two responses were both auspicious for their refusal to even discuss the idea. But suddenly, a strong voice spoke out, "If we DON'T do this, I'm outta here!" "I'll be gone, too," said another. And so the family of twelve moved into the undercroft for the summer. The vicar, determined to know as much as possible of the ways and traditions of these folks, had discovered that regular worship on Sunday mornings was not a big deal in their lives, though they *were* in church on every high holy day. And they were delighted to have the mama and papa finally married, the babies baptized, and the entire family became "members" of the church.

It's a comfortable parish; comfortable with itself and who it is and is likely going to be, because a declining population in the community is not likely to see lots of new members coming down the road. Then there's the "Red Roof Inn." The vicar says it's an informal designation by necessity, as they have not sought permission from the parent company. The sign beside the door into the parish hall, however, names it very precisely. There it hangs awaiting community gatherings, as event space is at a premium in this tiny town. "I don't get to count these people in my Sunday attendance records," the vicar smiled, "but they are sure extended family to everyone here. There's always room for Jesus, whatever church He might come from," he added. There've been prom breakfasts, wedding receptions, family reunions, scout troops, almost every kind of gathering that can be named has called the "Red Roof Inn" home.

In Newport, Kentucky, there's a food pantry that began a few years ago at St. Paul's, an historic parish on the banks of the Ohio River. St. Paul's sits in an area of the suburbs of Cincinnati where apartment dwellers abound and business areas are being reclaimed. The ministry, which started as a gleam in the eye of the rector and a few members, has evolved into a thriving ministry that is counted on by the city and draws volunteers from across the area.

In Kansas, there's a small church that facilitates distribution of foods that arrive in bulk from Kansas City. There are two huge needs to be taken care of before that food can reach the people who need it: turning the bulk goods into individual packets, and actually distributing the individual meals to real people. Church members volunteer to create the individual portions, and then to stand in a parking lot, whether in blazing heat or the cold of a winter blizzard, to see that people who need this precious food get it.

What does it take to be the church?

Often, awareness and willingness.

Lessons on faithfulness #9

"The cost and the promise . . ."

For discussion

"Life together is not to be confused with a romantic sense of community. The Christian community exists for the sake of the world. It is the difference between being church and doing church."
–S. Michael Craven[2]

---

2. thinkexist.com

- **For personal reflection:** Have you ever been the church in someone else's eyes? When and how?

- **For group reflection:** How are you the church in your community outside of worship?

- **For action:** What might you do this week to take the church to someone who needs it?

CHAPTER TEN

Jello Salad,
the Cookie Lady, and
Urban Neighborhoods

*The village in our mind
may develop and survive in
the midst of a large city.*
PETER MEGARGEE BROWN[1]

Small communities don't just exist in small towns and villages, but can also be enclaves on the outskirts of cities and larger towns. Such a place is the community of Florence, Kentucky, just south of Cincinnati. Like many Episcopal churches, the small concrete block and brick building sits at an angle on a street even the bishop can't always find when he makes his visitation. A new parish hall has replaced the old basement gathering place. An unchanging aspect of Grace Church is its food: generous and hearty servings of baked ham, scratch macaroni and cheese, jello and fruit salads, and the cookie lady, with her infamous brown take-home bags of homemade cookies for the kids and kids-at-heart. Newer are the Bible study groups, led by the new young priest who has made his way up I-75 from Emory.

In a suburb of a western city, the average age at St. P's is sixty-five plus. The same is true of most of the neighborhood in a

---

1. Peter Megargee Brown, *Village: Where to Live and How to Live* (New York: Benchmark Press, 1997).

declining inner-ring suburb. Members of St. S's worship in a space that is too big for their small congregation, but full of nostalgia for the fullness that once was. It's too soon to know if big grants to organizations devoted to working with seniors will make a substantial difference, too soon to know if the slow influx of professional couples and families who like the urban neighborhood ambiance will help write a new story for this parish, or whether, somewhere down the road, this will turn into hospice care and a "good goodbye" to the church itself.

In the meantime, the acoustically alive space, with its room for musicians to set up, has become a great Wednesday night venue for performances. There's an open mike night, and there have been rising stars perform here, from a country music singer to songwriters. CDs are produced, and a happy crowd of listeners put money in a jar to retrieve their copies. "Penetrating the neighborhood is slow," says Ben, "but more people are coming each month. The musicians love the space and the people love them, so everyone is happy. Do they show up in the pews on Sunday? Not really, but I suspect the enjoyment of music and fellowship is a holy thing in its own right." In the meantime, there are twinkle lights around the altar area and green plants on the wide chancel steps. In some ways the Wednesday evening music is forever a part of worship in that space, and there is huge potential for other things that can happen here.

Just up the street, there is a retirement home housing two hundred fifty people. At St. L's, the younger folks in the congregation sang "Happy Birthday" at Sunday breakfast to a parishioner celebrating ninety-five years. "As far as I know," Ben reflects, "the only service at that retirement home is Roman Catholic and takes place once a month. Supposedly there are no Episcopalians or Lutherans there. It makes sense to offer a Eucharist there. We're working on the logistics."[2]

Ben is keenly aware of the demographics of his congregation, and the neighborhood; aware that change in demographic, *if* it

---

2. Telephone interview, March 25, 2014.

comes, will be slow, and many of the people now in this congregation will not be alive for the change. He is equally clear that a call such as his, to be present with these people at this time, in what could be the twilight of their church as well as their lives, is a significant and holy calling that has nothing to do with average Sunday attendance and everything to do with a spring of living water welling up to eternal life.

At St. T's in a western city, members of the parish have busy evenings serving donuts at a laundromat where college students and young professionals from nearby apartment complexes do their laundry.

Some folks remember that several decades ago, and a long time before, there was an historic church in downtown that sat in the shadow of larger protestant, almost-megachurches, land-locked and in need of structural repair. The property was sold and land was purchased at an exit off the interstate where now there stands a colonial-style structure that looks, they say, more protestant than Anglican, both inside and out. The wide open sanctuary, however, light filled, with walls that invite decoration and comfortable chairs that are interlocked and moveable, and the creative thinking of its priest and members have become home base to "Second Sundays," where art and science open the doors to the community of Madison County and beyond. Singers, blue-grass groups, scientists, art shows . . . all bring the message of the Gospel and the invitation of the Eucharist down from the altar and through the open doors.

In the Ohio River Valley, St. C's Church is located in a white flight neighborhood. "I inherited exhaustion," the priest says quietly. "They had been in survival mode too long. I knew they were pleased that I was there; pleased that the diocese was putting some focus, including dollars, into this place. But they weren't sure, and they weren't going to reflect huge joy until they could tell whether I was in this for the long haul, and whether or not anyone else, like the diocese, cared."[3]

---

3. Telephone interview, March 24, 2014.

Mike's own personal passion and energy for the work were all he had to go on in the early days. That commitment took him out to become the chaplain for the fire department; he was seen refereeing football games, as the home scorer at high school basketball games, on the community ethics board, walking the town and getting acquainted with the business people, and long before it was an in-the-news thing, doing "ashes to go." It wasn't long before exhaustion gave way to enthusiasm, and St. M's was writing grants to open a food pantry, which currently serves 800–1,000 people weekly.

Mike is blunt about the requirements for clergy. "Even if you feel called to this kind of parish, it's a roll-your-sleeves-up, get-your-hands-dirty kind of ministry," he states. "I can't expect anyone to follow me if I am not following the call to serve others beyond ourselves. I can't expect a group that has never done anything radical in ministry to march into my office and insist that they have a mission to do. I can put some options out there and show people that I am willing to put myself on the line."[4]

Narcotics Anonymous, Al-Anon, and AA have found a home at St. A's in a northeastern diocese. A support group that focuses on relationship issues, particularly grief after broken nonmarital relationships, is emerging in a city neighborhood. "It *is* church for us,' says the quasi-leader. "It's that important to the lives of a number of people."

Several decades ago, a magazine named *Lear's* was published, often depicting life in cities around the country. One memorable holiday issue featured pictures of groups that, upon first glance, appeared to be nuclear family groupings. On closer examination, it was clear that these were nontraditional groupings, ranging from professional colleagues to residents of an apartment complex who had become friends and as the magazine described, "funny family" to each other. The pages flashed before my mind's eye as I was listening to the stories from city neighborhoods, where isolationism and loneliness can take different forms than

---

4. Telephone interview, March 24, 2014.

it does in remote and distant smaller places. Church may already be taking new and different forms in these locations in response to these needs.

There is room for more!

Lessons on faithfulness #10

God touches differing hearts in new and different ways.

For discussion

"For I know the plans I have for you, declares the Lord; Plans to prosper you and not to harm you, plans to give you hope and a future." –Jeremiah 29:11

- **For personal reflection**: Have you ever been a part of a small neighborhood church in a city? What made it stand out for you? What were its challenges?

- **For group reflection:** What are some of the most creative minis- tries you know of in city neighborhood churches?

- **For action:** What might I do to learn about opportunities to serve in these areas near me? To serve?

CHAPTER ELEVEN

The Words of My Mouth, the Meditation of Our Hearts . . . and Is Julie Sick?

For this fragile time in history,
this tender and fleeting moment
of our lives, I am your priest;
God has called me to lead this
flock. As I look out this morning,
my heart has a wish list for you.

JAN KARON[1]

"Four people came up to me on Sunday after the service. Each one said that they knew that I was preaching directly to them," says Ben. "There's always a pastoral dimension to a sermon. I never use names. But of course, in a small congregation, I know exactly what is going on in people's lives, and they know that I know that."[2]

One of the realities of a small congregation is the more intimate knowledge of each other's lives. The daily, practical lives of the households that make up a congregation, as well as the big celebrations and crises, are seldom a secret from the members,

---

1. Jan Karon, *A New Song* (New York: Viking, 1999).
2. Telephone interview, March 25, 2014.

who are ready with prayers and casseroles, and are part of the relationship between priest and communicant. "The preaching comes from a profoundly intimate place," agree those who serve these parishes.

Those who gather for worship may be as few as a dozen, or swell to a "crowd" of fifty plus on a high holy day. "Without fail, when the worship starts, it doesn't matter how many are there. If it is happening in the Spirit, there is a whole crowd of witnesses who are fed, and inspired to go live the Gospel in some way," says Ben, adding, "Sometimes, when I hear people talking about numbers, comparing their ASA with someone else's, I wonder, did Jesus care how many were there when He spoke? I believe that it is possible for a small group of people to have an authentic encounter with the Divine, speaking to each other, looking in each other's eyes. There is an intimacy of encounter in that kind of group that brings home the truth that God really knows my name."[3]

Phillip, speaking from New England, where some would say the church is truly dying, says, "There are two high points in my life as a priest. They came from words that were said to me which made me know that at least for these two people, I had lived into what I was called to do as a priest. One man said, 'Thank you for letting me know that God loves me.'"[4] Phillip knew that experience from the inside out, having yearned for connection with people as well as God, and having found it in small churches. He is aware that most people don't believe that God does love them, and that truth is incarnated in the relationships of a small church.

Richard came to the Episcopal Church as an adult, after years away from organized religion. His was a token attendance for a number of years, a bit of placating a new wife, who happened to be a lifelong Episcopalian. They visited several large congregations, whose choirs and adult formation programs were an incentive for her, but not for him. They had begun attending a pastoral sized congregation where he was immediately struck by

---

3. Interview, May 27, 2014.
4. Interview, May 27, 2014.

the personal style of preaching, and the good-natured fellowship. He would have assessed himself as very much on the "outside" of parish life when a family illness called him out of state for several weeks.

To his amazement, there was a group phone call from a church event, with a cell phone passed around the room while everyone inquired how things were going and told him he was missed. "When I got back," he says, "I *knew* without a doubt that the very first sermon was directed at me. I knew the priest knew what I had been going through, and the words that morning were exactly what I needed to hear."[5]

"When clergy gather, there's always a lot of conversation about ASA," says Ben. "I hear people talk about looking out at empty pews, or how full the church is. When I am in the pulpit or behind the altar, looking out at the congregation, I don't see empty pews. I see that Julie's seat is empty, and I wonder if she is sick. Carl's not there. Did things get worse at home? It's a really deeply personal taking in of who is present and who is not."[6]

Karl Vaters says, "Because I pastor a small church, I don't speak to a crowd, I preach to individuals. I know some very deep things about most of the people sitting in front of me. Some deep, dark things and some deep, wonderful things. While I don't bring up those intimate issues when I preach, the fact that I know them gives my messages a poignancy that can't exist in the most eloquent of messages preached to a nameless crowd or to people watching on a screen in another room or on the internet at home."[7]

It's personal. The small church is personal.

Getting an appointment with the rector is generally an easy task. You know each other personally. The waiting line is not so long that you can't get in for two weeks or a month. He or she may already know at least part of the reason that you want to

5. Interview, May 9, 2014.
6. Telephone interview, March 25, 2014.
7. Vaters, *The Grasshopper Myth*, 75.

see them. In some small churches, the rector or vicar keeps their own appointments; it's a matter of catching them at the office or on the cell phone to schedule a time. Others might have the assistance of a part-time secretary or parish coordinator, who is in charge of scheduling all appointments. Wait time is generally short, and unless a congregant is very new to the town or congregation, will be welcomed by name by both the priest and anyone else who happens to be in the vicinity when they arrive. The down side for the small church is the reality that in one-man and one-woman shows, or when a priest is a circuit rider serving three or four congregations, someone is not always accessible in the office to see folks, and the cell phone voicemail is likely to be the "secretary."

The same is true for attendance. Empty seats are not about ASA. They are question marks regarding someone's health and well-being, for it is unusual for folks to be missing on Sunday without letting someone know where they will be. "If someone is not there, and they didn't say they were going someplace this weekend, they'll get a phone call, checking to see if they're OK," says Martin of his small congregation. Men and women sharing the table at coffee hour glance at each other and then give Martin a nudge. "Tell her about Jesse." Martin shifts in his chair, looks down at his hands, and clears his throat a time or two before he begins to speak. The Jesse story is clearly not an easy one for him to recall.

"Jesse had always been in pretty good health," he begins. "He wasn't old, not by a long shot, just comfortably middle aged. One Sunday he wasn't feeling very good at church, and we all were encouraging him to go to the doctor. I thought I'd give him a day or two and check on him. The first time I called, he didn't pick up. So I called the next day. Same thing. When I didn't get a response on the third call, I thought I'd drive out to his farm and see if there was anything he needed."

Martin pauses. Swallows hard. And begins to speak again. "When I turned in to his place, I saw that mail was spilling out of the mailbox. No one had picked it up for several days. I started to get a terrible feeling—something was really wrong."[8]

Martin found his parishioner dead—and suspected he had been dead for several days. It's still a hard story for him to tell, but in his book, it's a good example of how these folks care for each other on an everyday basis. B.T. has been sitting quietly, listening to the conversation. Now he speaks up, adding his voice to the mix. His wife died a few years ago, he says, and he discovered at that time exactly how much this church did pay attention to what was happening in the lives of its people. "They were really there for me," he remembers.

Novelist Jan Karon hit the best-seller list for fiction with her Mitford series, stories about an Episcopal priest named Father Tim who has become the bane of many transition officers' and bishops' lives, for the false sense of reality about parish life and process, not to mention boundaries. Karon made a personal appearance at St. Francis in the Fields Episcopal Church near Louisville, Kentucky, on a spring Sunday. Her talk was slated for 4:00 p.m. Soon after morning services had ended, the spacious property around the church began filling up with cars of visitors who wanted to be sure they had a seat for the event. After the reading, a line snaked around the large parish hall, patiently waiting for a chance to shake hands with the author and receive a prepaid autographed book.

Covering the event for the diocesan paper, I made my way around the room, inquiring what had brought individuals to the event. They had come from every denomination, from churches large and small. Some identified themselves as "nones," who found themselves responding to these stories. The answers were of a kind: Mitford, Lord's Chapel, and Father Tim had touched some chord about what a church might be. It felt personal, they said. People knew each other. They cared. And they were known by their priest.

---

8. Interview, May 18, 2014.

Many attendees came from large urban congregations in the Louisville area. Others had traveled several hours from southern Indiana and central Kentucky for the afternoon. I knew all of the things that were out of kilter about Mitford, Lord's Chapel, and Father Tim. I knew the mythology that people were buying into was just that—a myth. And, I knew that I was experiencing a collective yearning for something that, for whatever reason, many churches were not offering.

These several decades later, listening to clergy of small churches speak about the personal nature of their ministries, and the personal context of their preaching, there was an echo of that afternoon.

To know and be known. Up close and personal.

Lesson in Faithfulness #11

There is a universal yearning to be known.

For discussion

"I felt as if she were speaking directly to me, as if she had seen inside my soul." –Anonymous

- **For personal reflection:** Have you ever felt that the words of a sermon were intended just for you? What was that like for you? Is personal connection with clergy and congregants important to you?

- **For group reflection:** How do you see the personal nature of a small church as an asset for the future of the church?

- **For action:** What has a sermon moved you to action on in the past several months? Share as much as you can regarding if and how you moved from being touched to thought process to action.

CHAPTER TWELVE

What's an Institution to Do? From ASA Snobbery to Hope for the Future

To make room for
something new to happen
is to see without filters.
CHARLOTTE KASL[1]

It is important at the conclusion of any research, quantitative or qualitative, to test the model for validity and reliability in the findings.

- Has the research and researcher been open to new concepts and willing to change his or her preconceptions if the data are not in agreement with them?

- Has the research and researcher been open to the fact that any topic of research is preliminary, and may change during the research process?

- Has the researcher collected data under the paradigm of structural variation of perspectives to avoid one-sidedness?

- Is the analysis directed toward the discovery of similarities?

---

1. Charlotte Sophia Kasl, *If the Buddha Got Stuck: The Handbook for Spiritual Change* (New York: Penguin, 2001), 93.

My original research topic began with the realization of lessons in faithfulness I had personally learned in my experience in small churches in our diocese. Was my experience simply that—my experience—or were others having such experiences and having learnings which were worthy of sharing with the wider community? That thread remained consistent throughout all interviews across the Church and the country. One conversation led to another, as numerous of those interviewed just "knew" someone whose small-church experiences needed to be included.

Unexpected threads were revealed in the interviews:

1. Discontinuity experienced in present seminary career-track training, pension fund structure, and the realities of a denomination of primarily pastoral sized congregations with specific needs.

2. The possibility that church growth of spiritual substance might become an articulated goal for all churches, allowing acceptance of the organically appropriate size, and preparation for the particular needs of the smaller church.

3. That in church life as in secular life, there are entities, which, for a variety of reasons, may over time no longer be viable. Effort must be expended to teach best practices in the adaptive challenges of mergers, creative partnerships, and where necessary, thorough preparation for hospice care and the healthiest possible closure.

4. An overview of the cultural evolution and parallels of church growth show the shift in population centers and movement from neighborhood, city, and rural churches to the suburban program and megachurches of today, with an emphasis on response to a consumer culture. A further look at the psychological and spiritual needs of individuals indicates a growing emphasis on building community and the desire for more close relationships, as well as dissatisfaction with religions that do not appear to live out what they claim to believe and teach.

Could it be possible that instead of following the culture and an infrastructure that no longer supports the reality of who we are, we might recognize the lessons in faithfulness we have to learn from these small churches? As this book goes to press, one more commission on the structure of the Church is trying to figure out how to rebuild the mother ship, an institution that Archbishop Desmond Tutu once called "totally untidy—and very, very lovable!" Out and about in the world, sociologists and psychologists are talking about the desires of people for communities where they know and are known. Folks who track the economy and jobs report that family farms are fading away, and firms that deal in technology, space science, and astrophysics are the wave of the future. At the same time, urban tribes, shared housing, and other groupings show the desire of people to be in relationship.

And the institutional powers that be continue to speak of merging dioceses and closing the doors of any congregation that has an average Sunday attendance under two hundred.

"The Episcopal Church gave up on small churches some years ago," says Phillip, a New England priest. "They thought the world was changing, and people didn't want or need neighborhood or small rural congregations. The way to keep up with the world was to have bigger churches with more 'opportunities,' a real consumer model that bet on people driving to get to larger churches with more to offer. The problem is, that had already been tried in England, and it had failed there. It's not working here."[2]

The questions posed to all individuals interviewed were: What do we as the institution need to do? What can we do?

The answers came in story form: stories that reveal characteristics of attitude, intentionality, and action—from the top. For that is who we are and how we operate at least for the present time and unforeseeable future. The stories also reveal a kind of denial about the reality of the demographics of this Church that indicate that facing the facts might be the first order of business.

---

2. Interview, May 27, 2014.

Bishops and bottom-line folks make a difference. Who are we going to educate and how we are going to educate? How can we restructure the pension program to reflect that great skills are needed in churches of *all* sizes, and that equitable distribution must be rethought if we are truly to have a church of the future?

Many local efforts at schools for ministry have proved unsatisfactory in producing the depth of formation hoped for. The possibility of regional schools and online offerings from seminaries gives hope for new opportunities for the formation of local and bi-vocational clergy. A part of it all, say seniors, must be "a new relationship between clergy and laity; new expectations of what each is responsible for." There also must be awareness of the critical nature of the situation and the matter of timing. Whether pursuing a traditional seminary education or an alternative form of preparation for ordination, the process takes three years of actual study, not counting the discernment process. One cannot identify the need one day and fill a position the next!

Will we try to hang on to the way it has been and the way the post-war corporate growth model led us, or recognize that there has been a tsunami and the landscape is not recognizable? The economic and cultural reality of our time has shifted. "The economy of scale really hurts small communities," says Bishop Lane of Maine. His description of the lack of tax base to support necessary services, industries, and young people leaving to go to the cities for work are echoed in the mountains of Kentucky as well as across the Midwestern plains.

In many smaller places, buildings are a crushing financial burden eating up all available resources of money, time, and energy. Bishop after bishop acknowledges this poignant conundrum. Episcopalians love their buildings. Much history and identity are connected to them, making it difficult to imagine worshipping in rented space, home churches, or other unexplored options.

In this bizarre, strange land of the twenty-first century, we have to think of new ways and try new things, and some of them might be reminiscent of something we had forgotten, or failed to value.

Russell H. Conwell, founder and president of Temple University, said it over a century ago in a lecture he gave across the world, entitled "Acres of Diamonds." Throughout the lecture, stories of individuals who, in search of diamonds (or silver or gold), which would make them wealthy, sold their land to go in search of that commodity. Some lost their lives in the search; most lost what possessions they had. And in each story, the person who had purchased their original property discovered "acres of diamonds" right there, where the search began.

Conwell ends his lecture with this statement: "Greatness exists not in the holding of some future office, but really consists of doing great deeds with little means and the accomplishment of vast purposes from the common ranks of life. To be great at all, one must be great here, now, in Philadelphia."[3] When he says "right here in Philadelphia," he means right here in your hometown, right here in Crosby's Corners, or Oshkosh, or Midvale.

We have "acres of diamonds" right here among us, in our small churches. Diamonds we have failed to see, with our sights set on something different, something more. In counting our treasures, they would not have been at the top of the list.

Bishop Lane adds, "As leaders, we have to recognize that our world has changed. The social contract no longer applies. The world has left us behind and we are scrambling to learn how to live and minister in its reality. If the future is in the small congregations, how do we get there?"[4]

In *The Grasshopper Myth*, Karl Vaters says, "The next step was to take our healthy church and make it a healthful one for others to gain nourishment from, not because we need greater numbers, but because our community needed greater hope."[5]

If he is right—and I suspect he is—his is one of several voices that need to be heard. There are beginnings of personal and

---

3. Russell H. Conwell, *Acres of Diamonds* (Philadelphia: Executive Books, 2004).

4. Telephone interview, June 5, 2014.

5. Vaters, *The Grasshopper Myth*, 135.

corporate voices looking to the resources for good lives in smaller places.

Can we hear them?

Perhaps this is one of the clues we have been searching for, that instead of following the cultural trends, we step out to lead in an area we do know something about—hope.

Perhaps it's time for all of the fine minds and top leadership who call themselves members of this Church to set aside business as usual and throw their imaginations and energy into something of promise—perhaps in a size and shape never imagined.

Lip service will not do any longer. A reality check says that if we were to close all congregations with an ASA under one hundred, we would wipe out 68 percent[6] of Episcopal churches in the United States. We can talk about those congregants finding their way into other churches that are larger, and more "successful" by budget and ASA.

Serving on the staff of a resource parish, a Christian Formation person with a background in psychology wondered about the time spent "allocating" what people *might* attend services at a particular time slot, if they had their druthers. "I felt like I was the crazy one, saying again and again, 'Do you *really* think that you are going to convince people for whom the nine o'clock service works best in terms of their family to come to another service because it would balance the attendance better?'" In places where landlocked small suburban parishes or rural parishes have been closed, statistics show that the former parishioners do not generally become active in program or resource parishes. Some fade into the numbers of "nones" who are not regular church attenders, or who drive long distances to another small church—Episcopal if they can find it, but not always so. There are groups of the former congregation that continue to gather annually to remember the stories, still offering support to each other across the years. Church members are not chess pieces that can be moved around

---

6. Mary Frances Scjonberg, *Episcopal News Service*, November 4, 2011, www.cpg.org.

the board to balance things out in the way statisticians, church growth, and financial folks wish. They are real, living, breathing people who have some personal preferences about church.

In 2008, the median of Episcopal churches in the United States showed an active membership of 164, with an average Sunday attendance of 69. In 2009, 50.7 percent of Episcopal churches had an average Sunday attendance of 66 or less; 57 percent had 200 members or less; 67 percent had 100 members or less. These statistics reflect Pew research data on ASA from all non-Roman Catholic Churches.[7]

The question then becomes, if 80 percent of Episcopal churches have an average Sunday attendance of less that 151, and re-structuring folks like to talk about closing any church with under 200 ASA, what will remain of the Episcopal Church? As more than one bishop said, if we close small churches, we won't *have* a church!

So *facing facts of who we are* seems to me to be the number one issue facing the institution in order to make any kind of effective decisions. Numbers alone will not get the job done. I suggest gigantic field trips of all who serve on structure commissions and other decision-making bodies. The diocese probably doesn't make a difference, as we all have our share of family and pastoral sized parishes. But the *requirement* should be that if one is to serve on a decision-making body of the Episcopal Church, they have to spend some time worshipping in small churches both in their own and other dioceses, visiting in the neighborhoods and communities that are homes to those churches, and talking with the clergy, vestries, and members to learn what life in the majority of the Episcopal Church is really like. They need to drive on the back roads as well as the interstates, and regain a sense of who the people of our country are and how all of them actually live.

On a recent trip on state Highway 62 in Ohio, after noticing a number of churches dotting the landscape, I decided to take an inventory in twenty-five mile increments. The highway meanders

---

7. Episcopal Domestic Fast Fact Trends, 2008–2012, episcopalchurch.org

through small towns with their requisite fast food and discount store outskirts and back into the countryside again. Without ever turning off the main highway, the smallest number of churches encountered was eleven. Full Gospel. Baptist. Methodist. Presbyterian. Christian. Roman Catholic. Friends. Episcopal. New Hope storefront. Does anyone see them?

Ralph, a New England priest, recalled a conversation he had on this subject with Diana Butler Bass, as they discussed the anomaly of the Baby Boomer days, when both attendance and giving were at a high level. "She said that we were coming back close to historical levels. Those high levels had never been the norm. But what she made me aware of is that the anomaly is what people have in their memories, not the historic trajectory. That makes it hard to accept that this *is* who we are. But it *is*."[8]

Number two would be *attitude*. Collectively, we must own that attitudes toward small churches have not been respectful. Many have had to put up with dysfunctional leadership in an outmoded deployment system that simply aimed for a warm body in congregations. "Often," said one priest, "the person in leadership has needed more care than they are able to give service. That can create innumerable other issues, which, when seen from the outside, make it look like a 'problem parish.' We have relied on people who we could get to go to hard-to-fill locations, and sighed with relief when the situation was 'covered.'"

The intent was never to do harm. But intent does not change impact, and the collective impact is of distrust and alienation from the system. It was often mentioned that most bishops do not make a clean jump from a family or pastoral sized parish to the head of a diocese, nor deans to head cathedrals, nor cardinal rectors. Many have never served in anything other than program or resource/cathedral sized congregations. Some attitudes, therefore, may be based in large part on limited personal experience of church, and programming of an institution that teaches that bigger is better and that rewards economically for climbing

---

8. Telephone interview, June 10, 2014.

the corporate (ecclesiastical) ladder. Ours has not been a system where large and small congregations are routinely partnered for long-term relationships and resources. And each bishop must face the bottom line in their diocese and try to figure out how to make it all work.

I believe this is one of many areas in which we are called to be truly countercultural, to defy the Madison Avenue PR types who push those "Bigger *Is* Better, Right?" ads, and start to really step back and take another look at "small" or "normal" before we begin allocating resources, both human and monetary. Instead of focusing on the corporate growth model that has been around since post-war (and to see that its time has come and gone), we could take the risk of stepping out ahead of the crowd, listening to those young adults as well as the sociologists who tell us that there are different values out there today—values that we should be uniquely equipped to handle *if* we stop trying to cram the square pegs of uniqueness into the only round hole we know.

What would that shift in attitude look like? Once again, the stories are rich. The bishop who, recognizing that isolation from large urban centers was a problem for keeping good clergy in rural areas, made it a point quarterly to use discretionary monies to bring clergy and their spouses/partners to the see city for a weekend, which was mostly for their refreshment and renewal. For at least a couple of times a year, the bishop saw several couples or individuals in town at the same time, to promote collegiality, and lessen the cultural and other forms of isolation.

Attitude

In order to keep good clergy in isolated areas, I/we must offer significant support and show awareness of key issues.

Regardless of their own academic backgrounds and pressures from academically minded clergy in their dioceses, Commission on Ministry members—both lay and clergy—need to understand the need for alternative types of formation for sacramentalists, preachers, and bi-vocational clergy, and provide support to this critical group that just might help save the church—both ours and others. Said Bill, "There were good things about the old Canon 9, when the plan was followed, which included good training, mentoring, ongoing continuing ed, and supervision. Where that was provided, good things happened. When it was not provided and a person was simply turned out to go do their thing without any guidance, of course it didn't work!"[9]

"We are not saying that we want to stop educating our clergy, or accept uneducated or undereducated clergy," said one bishop. "It is simply a fact that in today's world, we cannot expect that the three-year residential seminary experience is going to work for all of the people we need to fill all of our pulpits."[10]

Bring the clergy of large churches into the smaller churches, neighborhoods, and communities to experience the ministry done in these areas, and perhaps begin to build relationships that will lead to partnering between small and large, pulpit swaps, and sharing of resources. In several dioceses, churches (which share a name) "find" each other and build on that shared identity. In one diocese, the bishop sponsored a clergy mission trip into a more isolated part of the state, building in "show and tell" from the congregations, lunch or dinner with the congregants, and actual work in the communities. "I really resisted going," said one priest, "and I think it was one of the best things I've done in my ordained life. I learned *so* much! I had no idea how much could be done by so few people, with what my vestry would consider limited resources. I'm hoping to really build on this experience."[11]

Intentionality and Follow-Through

These were suggested by numerous people, lay and ordained. They are tired of lip service, promises, and no actual follow-through people-to-people, and often no follow-through when

---

9. Interview, May 14, 2014.
10. Telephone interview, September 11, 2014.
11. Interview, July 23, 2014.

financial help was promised. One resource parish received major diocesan hype for "adopting" a smaller parish, which included helping support the work of a deacon in that church and sending small groups from the congregation to worship periodically the two and a half hours from the urban center. The real story is of only two years of a three-year commitment funded, and very few visits by the communicants of the larger church to the small. Intentionality and follow-through are needed on part of both bishop and rector!

On the other hand, a bishop and staff were intentional in scheduling diocesan training events in rural and smaller locations as well as in the city and larger congregations, *and* in strongly encouraging key clergy from larger congregations to attend events in those outlying areas. The impact in terms of relationship building and connectivity within the diocesan family continues to be significant.

Tell the Story

The story of the smaller Episcopal churches often does not get the exposure given to the churches with larger resources and larger "events" and services. Again and again both lay and ordained spoke of intentionality in regularly featuring smaller churches in publications and on websites so that their stories are known. In one diocese, every congregation, regardless of size, is asked to submit exactly the same information for the e-newsletter, which will be posted the week prior to the bishop's visitation. No ASA or parochial report-type info.

- Submission #1. An article reflecting on "What is God up to at St. A? Where do you see that reflected?"

- Submission #2. Pictures that reflect the answer to #1.

- Submission #3. A short reflective piece by the rector or priest-in-charge, and a picture to accompany it.

The series has been tremendously popular, and is beginning to make the small churches feel good about themselves, hopefully educating the clergy and laity of the larger churches about the ministry that can happen "wherever two or three are gathered." This kind of intentionality is important for the self-esteem of the small congregations. As Phillip said, "They have a profound faith in God; they don't always have enough in themselves."[12]

Serious Reallocation of Resources

The system of the Episcopal Church is caught in a never-ending loop of seeing program to corporate sized parishes as successful, and rewarding top pensions based on the top salaries paid in those parishes, as well as for the administrative costs of diocesan life.

In the diocese of Western Kansas, Bishop Mike Milliken and Carl, a senior cleric, proposed to a CREDO gathering that if they were really serious about listening for God's call, they would share resources to the extent that all retirements would be equal; that no one would be punished at retirement because their call from God was to ministry in a small and less well-resourced church. The suggestion was resoundingly poo-pooed. This story came back to haunt me as I listened to an NPR report regarding teachers and the effort to eliminate a system whereby ineffective teachers are tenured, often in the less-well-resourced schools. "We should be putting our best and our brightest in these tough situations," the impassioned speaker was saying, "where they have a chance to turn things around; to really *do* something!" All too often, the wisdom about such assignment of talent and resource is named, but sadly nothing is done to see that the idea becomes reality, in education or the Church.

In the Diocese of Southwestern Virginia, there was a resolution before Diocesan Convention that all clergy receive the same pay, based on their experience, regardless of the size of the congregation. The resolution is presently tabled and "under study." Said a priest, "We can say the corporate model as the aspiration for the theological equivalent of the 'corner office' is dying, but it will

---

12. Interview, May 27, 2014.

leave kicking and screaming. And I'm still not sure what any of it has to do with the Gospel of Jesus Christ."[13]

A report from the gathering of the Bishops of Small Dioceses says that a representative from the Church Pension Group wants to meet with them to "pick their brains" on what might be done for nonstipendiary clergy, as their services are needed more and more. "At least we're beginning the conversation," he said.[14]

A serious reallocation of both human and financial resources must be considered if we are to remain a viable institution. Karl Vaters states unequivocally that "Joel Osteen could not do my job, and I could not do his."[15] His point is that there are different and equally valid calls to churches of different and equally valid size. However, little respect is given to either the small churches or the small church pastors—and that has to change.

It's *not* a quick fix, by a long shot. It's a lumbering old system, and we've become accustomed to what it's *supposed* to be like, both in the Church and the culture.

Writing on small church ministry for *Vestry Papers*, Lindsay Hardin Freeman says, "There are a few myths floating around about small congregations: they reflect the demise of the Church; they are poor; they are troublesome; and they are a minority in the Episcopal Church. As with churches of any size, some of those things may occasionally be true, but the point about small churches being a minority is *not* the case. Half of our congregations are small or family sized congregations, where ASA is seventy people or less. Another 29 percent of our congregations report attendance from 71–150 people. So, some 80 percent of our congregations have less that 151 people in worship on a typical Sunday. While 150 may be a large number by some standards, it is modest by most, where, large or small, stability and growth is achieved by reaching the hearts and souls of each person, through one-on-one work, small groups, good preaching,

---

13. Interview, September 13, 2014.
14. Telephone interview, September 11, 2014.
15. Vaters, *The Grasshopper Myth*, 8.

or outreach. Bottom line: it's about Jesus. Is He present and are people in touch with and moved by Him? Does that knowledge make a difference and does it change lives of those in the Church and in the community? Size is not a predicator of success or failure. What predicts such outcomes are the factors above. And while the checkbook balance in small places probably has less cushion than in larger parishes, what smaller churches *do* have is this: the close-to-the-heart knowledge that the smallest community of all—the twelve disciples around Jesus—formed the body that changed the world."[16]

We have become numbers snobs, and our attitudes reflect that snobbery. We are so busy looking at bottom lines and ASAs that we miss the Kingdom examples among us. We don't have metrics for health-full-ness or measures for faithfulness. But we do have descriptions of the qualities that those who live and work in small churches offer again and again to describe who they are.

The Core

Every church has a core group to some extent who are simply *there*, and will not be going elsewhere. It is possible in larger churches for this core group to be swallowed up by the larger churn of coming and going that is typical in the program and corporate parishes. In smaller congregations, particularly in more rural or isolated parts of a diocese, there is a sense of: we are here and we will always be here. In some locations, it's because there is not another Episcopal option, nowhere else to go, so there is a sense that things must be worked out with the people at hand.

"It's a 'grow where you're planted' thing that I leaned from a small church," says Ralph, looking back at what he calls one of his most formative experiences as a priest. "There's a wisdom to that. The next town over doesn't have more answers than you do. Whatever answers we're going to find are going to come right

---

16. www.ecfvp.org/vestrypapers/small-church-ministry/editors-note/

here, even if it doesn't look like what you want." Can it become toxic? Of course, no matter the size of the church. But here is where health-full comes in.

Church Matters

"One of the most important things I learned in a small church was how much church, and God, and faith matter," says Ralph. "People never hesitated to ask for laying-on-of-hands or prayers before surgery; they wanted it; they needed it. They showed up. They came on Sunday. They came on Wednesday nights to pray, even if there were just two or three of us. It wasn't a social nicety or something optional. It really mattered. It was a huge part of their lives."[17]

Jack, a product of a small church prior to seminary, whose field education and first call to a parish found him in corporate/resource sized congregations, says, "It hit me that one of the differences in a large church and a pastoral sized is that it's easy for there to be a complete separation, a 'behind closed doors' kind of actuality in a large parish, where there is absolutely no sense of how things get done. It's all done by staff, with the members by and large benefiting from the result of that work by the staff. The staff itself is constantly aware of the competition down the street, and how to market what they're doing. We must keep up with the 'Joneses' and their 'product.' In the normal sized congregation, people *know* how things get done because they are doing them, not just consuming them, or observing them."[18]

Relational

Perhaps one of the greatest resources of the small church is its relational base. The people of small churches are connected to each other. The possibility of intimacy exists. "All spiritual matters are

---

17. Telephone interview, June 10, 2014.
18. Interview, September 13, 2014.

matters of connectedness,"[19] says the Rev. Stuart Hoke, retired professor of Pastoral Theology at General Seminary, now enjoying serving many small congregations in the Diocese of North Carolina. "And these churches are relational; connected."

"Small churches are about people and relationships, not numbers,"[20] says the Venerable Bryant Kibler, who has served small parishes and is now president of the Mountain Grace organization,[21] as well as serving two small churches in the Diocese of Lexington.

Alice, a postulant doing fieldwork in small parishes after serving as lay staff in resource churches of two denominations, sees the future church in what she describes as "sheer faithfulness" and "real relationships." "It may not even be in a traditional building, but these people 'get it.'"

"What I learned in a small church," says Ralph thoughtfully, "is that it's all about relationships. We have it backward when we try to do program to build relationships. When the relationships are built, then the other stuff can happen. In a smaller place, the relationships are built and we see what grows out of them."[22]

Fellowship

It's hard to think of a small church without thinking fellowship. The crowd that gathers and grows as it makes its way to a local restaurant after Sunday services in Corbin. The wedding and baby showers. Casual or not-so-casual get-togethers in homes. Card groups. Movie groups.

Is this not a community to be grown, like the church of the Upper Room, as we rethink church and the use of buildings? Reflects one bishop, "We have a struggling congregation whose one-hundred-year-old beautiful building is eating them alive. They

---

19. Telephone interview, May 12, 2014.
20. Interview, May 14, 2014.
21. www.visit-eam.org/index.php/mountain-grace-conference
22. Telephone interview, June 10, 2014.

have a parish hall with a fantastic stone fireplace. With just a little adjustment and focus on the fireplace, it could become a center for fellowship in the town.[23]

Energy

Again and again, clergy who were supplying or working in small churches spoke of the energy that they experience. Since we often hear more about those small places that are on life support, perhaps near their last breath, with little or no energy for anything but trying to keep the doors open, I wanted to know more. A church without energy might be having some problems—and is generally considered a problem. A church where energy is a resource they want the rest of the Church to know about and learn from, that's a gift.

"What's its source?" I asked.

- Love—of God, the Church itself, and the rituals and traditions of the Church.

- The Holy Spirit. "Not to sound hokey or spooky or anything" said one cleric, "but they really do follow the lead of the Holy Spirit—they take it seriously—so for the most part, my energy follows theirs."

- Preaching. An appreciation for the Word.

- Fellowship opportunities. (Goes with being relational people.)

- Memories and stories.

- Pride in the Book of Common Prayer.

"Synergy," says Ann. "It happens between the priest and the lay leadership. Sometimes the vestry or the music committee energizes me, and sometimes I energize them. At our best, there is an equal flow of ideas, thinking and praying together. On Sunday

---

23. Telephone interview, September 11, 2014.

someone might say, 'Let's have a men's supper,' and someone else
says, 'Let's call the bishop and see if he might want to come,' and
by Wednesday, there are forty-five men gathered, and it all just
happened. When I was on the staff of a large church, that would
have gone before the staff for approval so we were all working
together and it fit with the rest of our programs. Here, the synergy
created it."[24]

"All too often the dioceses neglect the energy that is in these
places, because they are looking for different manifestations of
energy and success," said one senior clergy. "When the vitality,
the energy, the very real success in terms of faithfulness and ministry where they are planted are not recognized and honored, there
is a fear that 'the Diocese' and 'that bishop' are going to close
them, and anticipatory grief turns to sarcasm, anger, and greater
disconnect from the diocese."[25]

Appreciation

"I have never experienced greater appreciation than in the small
churches where I supply," says Tony. "Appreciation for the sacraments being made available. Appreciation for their church and
its traditions. It's a quality that is hard to describe and instantly
recognizable when you encounter it."[26]

Perseverance

Cornelia is a lively ninety-two years old, and still in love with the
small church where she and her husband worshipped together.
Over the years she has served in virtually every leadership position in the church. On this Sunday when the congregation is
welcoming a new priest-in-charge and lay associate, with ongoing
creative efforts for clergy leadership, she is effusive. She inspects

24. Telephone interview, June 11, 2014.
25. Telephone interview, May 12, 2014.
26. Telephone interview, May 12, 2014.

the landscaping to be sure nothing is amiss. She is a symbol of faithful perseverance.

"We are not quitters," says Jean, a long-time senior warden. "My turn to serve comes up every few years," she smiles, adding that between terms as an "official" of the congregation, "You just take on another job. It takes all of us to keep things going around here." Jean describes herself as something of a "bulldog." "I'm tough. I'm pretty tireless, and very determined."[27]

Listening to Jean, it occurred to me that every small church has at least one "bulldog." Sometimes, unfortunately, the bulldog can also be a bully, who, out of their own need to control things, intimidates others in the congregation. On the positive side, the tenacity of a bulldog has been and continues to be important to the stability of the congregation.

"Part of the perseverance is of finding their own niche in their local community," says Kibler. "People in Harlan, for instance, know that the Episcopal church in their community does things for the community, from hosting the ecumenical service to giving significant funds to the community medical center."[28]

Genuine

"We are who we are," says Marsha, at forty-seven one of the younger members of her congregation. "It's pretty hard to try to be someone you're not when everyone in town knows everything about you already if you've lived there a long time. If you have just moved to town, they'll soon learn the stories."[29]

"For the most part, we like each other," says Ted, a member of a small suburban congregation in New England. "I'd describe it as the kind of 'like' of extended family, where we know each other so well, that we know."[30]

---

27. Interview, May 12, 2014.
28. Interview, May 14, 2014.
29. Interview, May 15, 2014.
30. Telephone interview, May 16, 2014.

Thrifty Generosity

"People in the small congregations know how to get along with a little instead of a lot," says Bryant Kibler. "Their frontals and burses may not match, they might be hand-me-downs, but there is a sense that it is not the essence of who we are and what we do."[31]

Back in the days before the mountains were slashed, inviting folks in and out of the towns and villages, before the interstate highways crisscrossed our nation, and almost every area of a state might have a hairpin curve and two-lane roads where the shoulders almost weren't, and when meeting an oncoming car was occasion for driving almost into someone's field of tobacco or corn, small churches that were tucked into remote corners of rural areas were the backbone, the cultural and social centers of the place they were located. Their urban counterparts were based in neighborhoods where people walked to church as well as shopping. One congregation remembers a bishop who must have loved them a great deal, for he came to town for confirmations on Thursday and didn't go home until Monday. Never mind that the train schedule only allowed him traveling "to" on Thursday and "from" on Monday! The natural barriers, combined with communication by mail and the rarest of long-distance phone calls in pre-Internet and cell phone days, meant that the ties that bound a diocese were loose. They were dependent on the annual visitation to the parish and the gathering of the diocesan family at the yearly convention, when individuals or carloads went over or around those formidable mountains or traveled the narrow roads. Survival meant the development of a sturdy independence. Independence that *could* become isolationist. Isolationism also led to tolerance of behaviors that were neither attractive and appropriate nor likely to make anyone "know that we are Christians by our love."

---

31. Interview, May 14, 2014.

Before the skeptics start, let me make clear that I make these remarks with eyes wide open. I no more idealize the small church than I worship the large. There are examples aplenty of both that are not health-full or growth-full. They are not the ones of which I write.

Thom S. Rainer, in *The Autopsy of a Deceased Church*,[32] provides a list of the characteristics of churches that have died, churches of many sizes, locations, and denominations:

- The past was the hero; the "good old days" were typically twenty or more years in the past.

- The church refused to engage with the community; is not known in the community.

- The budget was inwardly focused.

- Prolonged times of apathy and internal conflict.

- The Great Commission became the Great Omission.

- Church members were overly focused on their own preferences.

- New members were rare.

- Pastoral tenures became shorter and shorter due to frustration and conflict.

- The congregation rarely prayed together.

- The congregation had no clear purpose.

- The congregation obsessed over the facilities.

These symptoms of illness can plague any size church; they are not limited to those that are "small" or "normal" in size. The good news is that across the country, there are small "normal" sized churches that are the antithesis of these symptoms— continuing to serve God, despite lack of respect and support from within the system.

---

32. Thomas S. Ranier, *Anatomy of a Deceased Church: 12 Ways to Keep Yours Alive* (Nashville: B&H, 2014).167

What could happen if we began to celebrate and support these, the majority of churches?

"It's all about people," says Ann. "It's about building relationships, about engaging in life with each other." She smiles impishly and imagines out loud what it would be like if all large churches were mandated to break into units of one hundred and fifty. "Imagine how we would double the size of our dioceses!" she exclaims. "These are the actual working sized units of most larger churches, and the maximum size of the pastoral sized."[33]

"Seriously, "she continues. "It's about something deeper than these units and numbers, I believe. I think it's about trading places in order to be in relationship, to know each other and each other's communities. What if I and my vestry and a group of people were to attend St. D's across the diocese from us, and the rector and vestry and some worshippers from St. D's were to come to our church? We need to get outside the way we've always done things and allow inspiration instead of institution to guide us, on behalf of not only our small congregations, but on behalf of the Kingdom of God. We've forgotten that the first disciples went out two by two—that's how they were sent. And as we begin to really engage with each other, not only will larger churches become resources for the small, but the small will become a resource for the large."[34]

I pray we begin.

A good starting place would be with the subtitle of Karl Vaters' book, *The Grasshopper Myth: Big Churches, Small Churches and the Small Thinking that Divides Us.*

---

33. Telephone interview, May 16, 2014.
34. Telephone interview, June 11, 2014.

Lesson on faithfulness #12

Yes, we *are* all in this together, and we really do need each other!

For discussion

Dear Lord and father of mankind, forgive our foolish ways!

- **For personal reflection:** As a member of a small church, what has been my assumption about large churches? As a member of a large church, what have been my assumptions about small churches?

- **For group reflection:** What myths about small churches have I de-mythologized and re-mythologized in reading and discussing this book?

- **For action:** If I am a small church person, what steps will I take to engage with and advocate for large churches? If I am a large church person, what steps will I take to engage with and advocate for small churches? Regardless of the size of my church, what can I personally do to raise the visibility and self-esteem of small churches?

Afterword

... two kinds of churches, two kinds of Christianity. One kind, Dober Street, supports people's customary and established ways of life and provides a chapel for their religious needs and rituals....

The other one, the Church of the Second Chance, challenges that same way of life and proposes an alternative. It is lived in community together." **ANTHONY B. ROBINSON**[1]

A sense of call, and willingness to step up to God's idea.

Caring. Commitment.

Love one another is bigger than we think.

Sing to the glory of God!

Extend the table.

Pioneer when it's called for.

Be the presence—God's face and hands and feet in the place you're planted.

Give your treasure away.

Balance tradition with newness.

Turn radical independence into interdependence; grow health-fully.

These are the essences of faith that stand out as I begin talking with ordained and lay men and women across the Church. As

---

1. Anthony B. Robinson, *Changing the Conversation: A Third Way for Congregations* (Grand Rapids, MI: Wm. B. Eerdmans, 2008).

with all qualitative research, there may well be additions as more stories are told.

The structures that form and send out the faithful of today with their stained glass windows, musical instruments, and steeples have long been our signs to the world that there are caring people and a larger purpose here. There are places where the size and weight of the structure is too large and too costly for the remnants who people the town or neighborhood these days. Signs have lost essential meaning to people who were not programmed by life to recognize them as beacons, or have been beat down by life in such a way that they no longer trust the signs or the stories and the life promise they represent.

We are called to conversation about what the church of today and tomorrow will be. It is a conversation taking place in a world of megas and maxis where it could be easy to forget "Wherever two or three are gathered in my name, I am there among them."[2] We have become so accustomed to the "bigger is better, right?" TV ads and attitudes that we seem to be unaware that relationships, which happen best in smaller configurations, are having a revival of focus, especially in the lives of young people, who crave foundational units of caring in their lives. Mid-lifers and seniors do, as well.

The voices that are not in this conversation tend to be not only the small churches themselves, but those who can talk *about* them from a perspective that is officially "outside" of each small community, yet connected by the ties of diocesan life, and an awe that comes from being exposed to the kind of faithfulness that is compelling. This kind of faithfulness is not about having to convince couples who want to rent the sanctuary that premarital counseling is important. It's not about professional choirs or professional educators. Sometimes it's not even about having "magic hands" available to make the Holy Eucharist possible.

It's about places that know from the inside out that the cycle of their lives are tied up with the essence of this place and its people.

---

2. Matthew 18:20.

It's about the healing service at Christ Church, Harlan, before seven-year-old Cade was off to Michigan for the too-many-eth heart surgery in his young life, where sixty-nine people showed up from the community. If the ritual was unfamiliar, Cade and his family were not. It's about the adopt-a-room-in-the-rectory program at St. John's, Corbin, where every single room was refurbished by a different family in the congregation, under the guidance of a skilled designer, to make it possible for a priest to come join in their community.

But it's far more than nice stories that touch the heart. It's about the qualities of life that are represented in the story that have an important message for those who hope for a future for the church. It's about how we make the attitudinal changes, which can only happen if our institutional practices encourage the respect for churches of all sizes, and recognize that growth of *the* Church and growth of a particular congregation are not the same thing.

Karl Vaters hits it on the head when he says, "My church isn't getting bigger. Not by Sunday morning attendance numbers. Statistically, we're one of those sad, under-achieving plateaued churches that cause denominational officials and church analysts to call emergency meetings to figure out how to fix us."

"But we don't need fixing, because we *are* growing. We have been for years now. The people in our church are happy and excited to get together, they're proud to bring their friends and family members with them."[3]

"Sometimes what we call a plateau is simply a church reaching its optimal size, and then using that size to grow healthful fruit. Not all growth is numerical. If you're in a church that is healthy, where people are growing in their faith, reaching the community, investing in missions and seeing transformed lives and families, it's shameful, even sinful to divert out limited attention, money, time, energy, and heart away from that into chasing numbers."[4]

---

3. Vaters, *The Grasshopper Myth*, 127.
4. *Ibid.*, 127.

David Kinnaman, president of the Barna Institute, says, "We should measure success not merely by the size of our church . . . but also by the depth and quality of spiritual growth in people's lives."[5]

It has often been said that when an idea surfaces in different contexts, shapes, and sizes across a wide territory, it may well be an idea whose time has come. Small or normal sized churches are everywhere. They may have not been speaking out in terms of advocacy for their kind; they're just busy *being* church, and *doing* church—growing the Kingdom. There are other small-in-number units in our culture that are speaking out, from homes for group living, to emergents and groups like the Presbyterian Ecclesia Project,[6] which sees 20s and 30s and 40s with their beliefs all over the place gathering in small Christian communities with areas of focus on lifestyle, forging covenant groups, designing creative worship, and recognizing that any time they spend together around a table is holy time.

Under current economic guidelines and institutional practices, the dream may not sound very realistic.

But the message is loud and clear.

It's time to legalize being small. To recognize, honor, and learn from those characteristics that, whether historic or emergent in nature, have something important to offer people—of all ages.

This means systemic change—and systems are lumbering creatures, hard to stop, difficult to steer in a new direction. But difficult is not impossible. In Christian lingo, it's about transformation, which is, after all, what we're called to do in the world.

So change must begin with us—each one of us, speaking out and living into respect for little things, little places, and little people—and the big lessons they have for us. It won't happen overnight. If it doesn't happen within our system, our system may well cease to exist, because its heartbeat will have, like Colleton, been destroyed as not worth saving.

---

5. *Ibid.*, 133.
6. Interview, April 2, 2014.

Faithfulness *is* the future, as it has been our heritage, one we have not always treated with respect.

Conclusion Rising

The conclusion to these thoughts announced itself in a place at once unlikely and oh-so-fittingly right: the weekday dimness of the largest cathedral of them all—St. John the Divine, sitting at the top of the hill in New York City's Morningside Heights. No description could have prepared me for the Phoenix sculptures that were soaring there, feat of both engineering and art. Twenty-two tons of birds, measuring ninety and one hundred feet in length.[7] From a distance, a fantasy of diverse textures and colorations. Up close, as the details emerged, it was possible to identify a body constructed of salvaged construction debris: pliers, saws, tubing, screwdrivers. Feathers made of carefully configured shovels. Crowns that were really used hard hats. Heads made of jackhammers.

In 2008, renowned Chinese sculptor Xu Bing was commissioned to build these creatures for the atrium of the World Financial Center in Beijing. Arriving at the site, he was shocked not only by what he perceived to be the outdated techniques and machinery, but the poor working conditions of the migrant workers. He determined to build his sculpture out of the detritus found at the site, materials that had been touched by these workers—a statement to all who would view it.

Officials who viewed the completed work were blind to the artist's vision. They feared that the raw, edgy phoenix would reflect poorly on Beijing during the Olympics. They asked Xu Bing to embellish the creatures with crystals, for a more impressive exterior. Xu Bing refused and moved the phoenix to another location. It was there that independent curator Judith Goldman saw them, and mindful of the Cathedral of St. John the Divine's

---

7. Carol Vogel, "Phoenixes Rise in China and Float in New York," *New York Times*, February 15, 2014, C1.

mission to invite and host discourse on topics important to the world, called the dean and told him about the opportunity to bring them to America, and to the cathedral, where they now fly hundreds of feet above the great worship space.

Writing in the *New York Times*, columnist Carol Vogel said, "They bear countless scars, they have lived through great hardships, but they still have self-respect. In general, the Phoenix express unrealized hopes and dreams."[8]

Moving the length of the cathedral, head tilted toward the suspended birds, the metaphors were clear. Xu Bing, who states that he wants people to understand the values the Phoenix represent to him, has taken that which others would consider too insignificant, too poor, too mundane, too small, and created entities of such beauty and power that we *must* stop to consider their meaning—for the Church, the world, the future.

The western myth of the phoenix is rebirth and resurrection. The phoenix lives for a thousand years, and then, his work done, builds a great fire, throws himself on it, and from the ashes arises a new young phoenix for a new time. In the Chinese myth, they are Feng and Huang, male and female, two in one, yin and yang.

Dean James Kowalski in a meditation on the Phoenix writes, "This is not simply political art. It is art at its best, educating our imagination as we understand better the way things are, and as we risk envisioning how they could be."[9]

Risk. Understand. Envision.

Times of great change, such as those in which we live today, are always times of risk. Perhaps the greatest risk is the set of questions that are raised, questions that must be answered by individuals and institutions.

What will it *mean* if we, too, shift the way we, like Xu Bing, see things that are small rather than large? Have been deemed insignificant rather than important? What kind of individual as well

---

8. *Ibid.*, C1.

9. "Dean's Meditation" in newsletter of the Cathedral of St. John the Divine, Spring 2014.

as corporate shift in values has to occur, and what impact might that shift have on individuals and institutions to admit that small is not always a problem to be fixed or a thing to be grown into a new size and shape to fit a predictable mold, but a container, as it is, for important life lessons?

How will we reflect on our own aspirations, dreams, choices, and journeys if the product needed for the hope of the future does not turn out to be the size we have always believed it to be?

Can we risk valuing the rose as much as the redwood? The hard hats, shovels, and scraps as much as the crystals? The storefront, chapel, or gathering place yet to come as much as the cathedral? The Kingdom Come Parkway as much as the Interstate?

For this is how it *could be*. The bishops, deans, and cardinal rectors, the great endowed spaces open to the qualities and values in the big lessons from the little places. All interacting with love and respect that honor the foundation that was trusted to only twelve—in order that we may, together, yin and yang, both/and—have a future for God in the world.

It is a risk we must take.

Lessons in faithfulness summary

*"To laugh is to risk appearing a fool; to weep is to risk appearing
    sentimental
To reach out to another is to risk involvement; to expose feelings
    is to risk exposing your true self
To place your ideas and dreams before a crowd is to risk their loss;
    to love is to risk not being loved in return
To live is to risk dying; to hope is to risk despair; to try is to risk
    failure
But risks must be taken because the greatest hazard in life is to
    risk nothing.
The person who risks nothing, does nothing, has nothing, is
    nothing
He may avoid suffering and sorrow, but cannot learn, feel, change,
    grow or live.
Claimed by his servitude he is a slave who has forfeited all freedom;
    only a person who risks is free*

*The pessimist complains about the wind; the optimist expects
   it to change
And the realist adjusts the sails."*
   –William Arthur Ward[10]

For discussion

- **For personal reflection:** What new awareness do I have about my assumptions about the size and ministry of both large and small churches? What is my greatest ah-ha?

- **For group reflection:** What new awareness do we have as a group about the importance of the both/and in terms of church size? The actual demographics of churches? Attitudes of both culture and institution?

- **For action:** What can I do to cultivate healthy churches in my own part of the world, and healthy relationships between churches of all sizes? What kinds of adaptive challenges are needed in the institution?

---

10. William Arthur Ward, www.goodreads.com/author/quotes

Bibliography

Brown, Peter Megargee. *Village: Where to Live and How to Live* (New York: Benchmark Press, 1997).

Chappell, Tom. *Managing Upside Down: The Seven Intentions of Values-Centered Leadership* (New York: William Morrow, 1999).

Conwell, Russell H. *Acres of Diamonds* (Philadelphia: Executive Books, 2004).

Dudley, Carl S. *Making the Small Church Effective* (Nashville: Abingdon Press, 1984).

Fox, John. *The Little Shepherd of Kingdom Come* (Lexington, KY: University Press of Kentucky, 1993).

Kasl, Charlotte Sophia. *If the Buddha Got Stuck: The Handbook for Spiritual Change* (New York: Penguin, 2001).

Lindvall, Michael L. *The Good News from North Haven: A Year in the Life of a Small Town* (New York: Crossroads Publishing, 2002).

Pappas, Anthony G. *Entering the World of the Small Church* (Washington, DC: Alban Institute, 1988).

Rainer, Thomas S. *Anatomy of a Deceased Church: 12 Ways to Keep Yours Alive* (Nashville: B&H, 2014).

Robinson, Anthony B. *Changing the Conversation: A Third Way for Congregations* (Grand Rapids, MI: Wm. B. Eerdmans, 2008).

Schaller, Lyle E. *The Small Church IS Different* (Nashville: Abington Press, 1982).

Vaters, Karl. *The Grasshopper Myth: Big Churches, Small Churches and the Small Thinking That Divides Us* (Fountain Valley, CA: New Small Church, 2013).